Paul B

Quit smc

Paul Bernard Gaspar

Quit smoking in 7 days

Independently published
2020

Publisher: Independently published

Quit smoking in 7 days / Paul Bernard Gaspar.

ISBN 9798624375284

CONTENT

ABOUT THE AUTHOR

I want us to become friends while you are reading this book. Quitting smoking is neither hard, nor impossible. As you need someone who constantly supports you in your hardest moments, I don't want us to be strangers while we go through this journey together. That is why I would like you to know a few things about me before embarking on our quest to quit smoking. This way you will get to know me better, you will feel familiar with who I am. You'll understand what I went through in my life as a smoker and my final struggle: how I managed to quit smoking. I will help you become receptive to my ideas shared with you in this book and you might notice that we went through the same, or at least similar, struggles.

Think of me as a friend who managed to quit smoking and who is now helping you to do the same thing through his own experience and advice. It is way easier to go through this struggle if you have someone beside you, so, I will follow you step by step and be present in your struggles through every word in this book.

I have been smoking for the most part of my life. Living in an Eastern European country, where selling cigarettes to kids is not monitored or controlled, I started smoking at the age of 14 and continued doing so for the next 15 years – this is way more time spent smoking than I have ever wanted and thought I would spend. The years have passed without me really noticing it; my money was burning with every smoked cigarette and my health was starting to damage. I didn't want to quit smoking for financial reasons only, but also because of the unbearable smell I was always leaving behind me. As a smoker you might know it is hard to run or do physical exercise after having a cigarette or two, so I started putting on a lot of weight and frustrated about my physical appearance, but did nothing to improve the situation, or at least to keep it under control. I had always preferred smoking instead of going to the gym so I spent a lot of time self-loathing.

As it was not enough, I was unlucky, so to say, to work alone at my online store. This allowed me the possibility to smoke continuously and unsupervised. No one was there to scold me or to open my eyes on the amount of cigarettes I was smoking.

Finally, I managed to quit smoking due to a long list of reasons, but the most important one was my fiancée. She never said that she was bothered by my habit, but I could read the disappointment in her eyes every time she was around me and saw me smoking. Maybe she was doing it without being aware, maybe she didn't want to impose rules in my lifestyle; nevertheless it bothered me seeing her unhappy because of my self-destructive habit. We both knew it was not healthy. She always encouraged me to quit smoking, but I simply couldn't. At a certain point, I started negotiating with her on how many cigarettes I was allowed to smoke: one cigarette after each meal, one during my morning coffee, one when I was stressed, and so on. I did manage to smoke less, but it still wasn't very helpful. Eventually, I ended up smoking the same amount of cigarettes I used to, but this time around I was hiding. This new excitement of not getting caught made me smoke even more. Although I felt guilty, I couldn't stop; I would have gone insane otherwise. My daily routine, work and life were hard enough and I just couldn't bear more anxiety and stress from quitting smoking...

The financial reason was also a motivation to quit smoking, but in the end, this still went down to my fiancée. Instead of spending money with her on romantic evenings, travelling, and building precious moments, I was spending the money on cigarettes.

On the one hand, my smoking habit was self-destructive; on the other hand, I was willingly smoking to destroy myself. Life's pressure was weighing me down. I felt overwhelmed with responsibilities, duties. I felt that I could not handle all of them, so I needed something to calm me down, to ease the pain in my life. Unfortunately, the only sedative I discovered in that period was tobacco. I played a kind of a Russian roulette: I could have died, but I also could have got away with it.

I didn't have any control over my life, and its uncertainties fuelled my self-destructive behavior.

I have been smoking for over 15 years, every day. I don't think there ever was a day I have not lit at least one up. Now that I think about it, there might be days during the many times I had tried quitting when I only lit a cigarette a day. Otherwise, I used to smoke about 40 cigarettes a day. The hundreds of times I tried to quit were doomed to failure. I was never really prepared. I never had the luck of reading such a book that would guide me, so I ended up failing every time; sometimes even half an hour after deciding to quit for good.

Sometimes I went through embarrassing moments. At school, when I didn't actually have any pocket money for buying cigarettes, I started lighting up other people's thrown away cigarette buds so I could be able to inhale some smoke. There were times when I was trying to inhale other people's exhaled smoke. I used to secretly smoke, hiding away from other people because I was afraid they would tell on me. Whether it was rainy or windy, snowy, cold or hot, I kept smoking. As long as I was getting my nicotine dose, nothing else mattered. Once I got really sick; I had some sort of a lung disease. Although my chest hurt every time I was inhaling, I continued to smoke carelessly. Maybe you have experienced similar moments. I just wanted to point out the critical situations a smoker creates when they is dependent on tobacco. You are not alone!

I hoped certain events would give me the impulse to change and quit smoking, but it never happened. It might have been possible, but my habit of coming up with excuses to be able to continue bad customs has chased it away. Sometimes I felt ill; I was tired. I felt as if my chest was pressing on to my lungs. I was coughing very badly and that was the exact moment I knew that I had to quit. I had been quite certain that I had to make that choice, but, until then, I wasn't able to follow through with it. Just the simple thought of quitting at that point made me anxious, so my brain used this as an excuse to continue smoking despite the heavy coughing. Any other opportunity to release myself from these shackles has been wasted.

I must admit, I did like smoking. I liked the taste of it, the smell, the feeling I got from exhaling it. At least, that's what I thought. At one point, I told myself I would continue smoking, but less and only light cigarettes. I kept telling myself that we should be able and allowed to do the things we like in life, and, unfortunately, I liked to smoke. That's how I managed to lie to myself, and I could only see these lies after so many lies, because at that point they came out as truths. Of course, I was wrong thinking that way. I would have been much happier and fulfilled if I had never smoked. This chain of events, or chains of various and complex information, have turned me into a non-smoker. Not suddenly, but progressively, I did realise I was wrong in excusing my smoking behave our all of the time and I also realised that everything that involves smoking and the joy of it, was actually a self-created illusion, a lie.

The reason I wrote this book was out of my own addiction to tobacco. When I finally decided to quit for good, I started doing my own research on why people say it is hard to quit. I was too afraid to try it on my own, again, so I needed to see if there was a possibility of cheating on the addiction. And there was, but the information was all spread out over the Internet and in books and it was rather incomplete. It is easier to quit smoking once you understand why you do it in the first place, what happens while you smoke, why you cannot stop, how your body is affected by this process and how nicotine creates a psychological addiction. I have always relied on my own potential to quit smoking anytime. This illusion stopped me from obtaining my goal of becoming a non-smoker. I knew what the key to quitting smoking was and this was exactly what made me think that I can do it anytime, but I never actually tried to do it. This way I kept pushing aside the actual moment I would quit; therefore, it never came. I was not as smart as I imagined. Potential remains only potential until you turn it into deeds. It doesn't matter how much you have the impression of knowing something, you will not accomplish anything until you act.

In the end, I realised I was deceiving myself. I always considered myself as strong and smart; traits I had never actually proven. This way, 15 years of my life have passed away, until I decided to take action so I could somehow compensate for all those last years that have been taken away by cigarettes. This problem had to be dealt with in order to face this physical and mental "disease" called "smoking".

INTRODUCTION

Know your enemies so you can know yourself better. Know yourself, so you can know your enemies better. Knowledge is the key. Self-knowledge will help you becoming a non-smoker. We are biological beings. We act upon built-in biological mechanisms, which we can luckily change. We react on internal impulses in ways we cannot imagine, and these reflect, in turn, upon our lives. Understanding these processes help us changing them; thus, it can lead in creating a better life for ourselves, one that we have control over.

One way or another, every smoker enters a state of panic each time the subject of quitting smoking is brought up. It's a natural phenomenon because our mind and body don't react well to sudden changes in our lifestyle, whether these changes might bear a positive or negative impact on our lives. Actually, the mind could make you believe that quitting smoking would negatively influence you: you will not handle the daily stress, you won't have any fun at parties anymore or you will not be able to focus on your tasks. Well, I can tell you now: this isn't the case, but you will understand this later on in this book.

I won't insist on the multitude of problems and diseases that smoking causes, but I have to at least mention some. We can't ignore them; maybe you didn't even hear about some of them. Through this book, I am seeking to prove you that it is possible to quit smoking without experiencing any pain, whether physical or psychological, and that you can quit in easy and pleasant ways, not through threats or stress.

Most methods and advice against smoking are either negative or they focus primarily on the fact that cigarettes are harmful, that they slowly kill you, inflicting painful and lethal diseases, that you lose money and smell bad because of them. We will not focus upon these aspects, but on what happens inside your body when you smoke and why. Then, we will focus on the optimistic part: how to quit for good. I am pretty sure you don't entirely understand what it means to smoke. I must admit: neither did I. In fact, nobody does unless they study it and this is your chance to get acquainted with the information. Truth be told, you need the information handed out to you. As long as you don't really understand the events that occur in your body and mind while you are smoking, you can't actually quit smoking without experiencing withdrawal. But once you have familiarized yourself with it, you will take an informed decision about whether you want to continue smoking or to quit for good. I am pretty sure it will be the latter, but it will be purely your own choice.

I understand your skepticism. In over 15 years of continuous smoking, it never came to my mind to read such a book. I mean I did think of it, but I couldn't actually believe it would help. How could it actually do any good if I simply read some lines in a book, when all that I feel is physical and real? Well, I was wrong. Just like a good psychiatrist helps people heal their trauma, books like this can heal your appetite for tobacco, help you get over the withdrawal and even make you despise smoking. Maybe you have tried quitting before and you believed that another try won't do you any good. It's ok to be sceptic; it can be quite productive sometimes if you use it in the right way. But it is also ok to try over and over again until you succeed. You will find all the information you need to become a non-smoker in this book. I have centralized and concentrated all the possible information regarding smoking that you need to quit it. Hundreds of ideas are present; my own life experiences and others' and lots of valuable data that will surely help you on your way to becoming a non-smoker. Maybe you will feel that this time it will be the same as before, but do not forget, if you step on grass multiple times, a path will be formed. And as long as you keep stepping on that small, newly-formed path, it will become wider and wider, and later on you will be able to see the way to your goal of quitting smoking even more clearly. I am sure the path is already there, in your mind. Now, with the help of this book, you will be stepping harder due to the new information you will learn. This time you won't be alone because I will be next to you. Not only we will make a path together, but a road in your mind, one that will be extremely easy to walk on, one that will lead you to a better, healthier and more fruitful life. All I can do up to this point is to encourage you to keep on reading this book until the end. Once you do, you will be convinced that I was only telling the truth.

Life is full of unforeseen events. Nowadays, everybody gives advice and tells other people how to live their lives. Everybody is a critic and everyone knows what's best for you, but nobody asks you what you actually want. You get opinions and recommendations on what to do through various forms, guidelines on how to actually live your own life. Everyone claims they are right, but who holds, in the end, the absolute truth? The answer and bearer of the absolute truth is: YOU, in your own reality where nobody should meddle. Your reality, as you perceive it, that only you can understand, and upon which only you can act, can be changed through action. But you cannot do it efficiently unless you know, somewhat, what is happening around you and without at least hearing other people's opinions. Although we should take decisions in life based on our own judgement, it is important to have all the information regarding a certain to pic before decide anything. Listen to what others have to say, including me, extract the information that suits you and judge only after carefully weighing the newly-found information with your own. Otherwise, you may only be a victim of your past influences and you risk engaging into a harmful undocumented decision. Judgement can be correct, false but also destructive, and in the latter case, due to misinformation, sometimes due to our own will, it can lead to destruction.

Do not let yourself be discouraged if you tried to quit smoking before and didn't succeed. Mark Twain once said "It's easy to quit smoking. I did it a hundred times". Each failure has brought you closer to your goal, your purpose. Don't look at this book with skepticism; it will only create a barrier between you and the newly-found information and you might fail because of it. You never know, this time it might actually work out for you and you will quit this harmful habit for good. Take the first step in quitting smoking by reading this book, and be receptive to the information presented. Then, be honest and ask yourself if you really want to quit smoking. Deep down in your soul, you know you want to. It's ok if you continue smoking while reading this book, no one asks you to instantly quit. I bet only the thought of you having to quit right now gives you the creeps. As I said, you don't have to quit now or while reading, only if you are really able to do it and focus on the rest of the book. As I am continuously talking about smoking in the book, it may be hard to resist the temptation. Please, don't react like Pavlov's dog each time I will mention the word "cigarette".

As you have to read with great care and understanding each word I say, so the information will print into your mind, we don't want to risk your thoughts be guided only towards smoking. However, I ask you not to read while actually smoking. You would defy everything I have written here and you will make your subconscious believe that your decision to quit isn't that serious. Don't alarm yourself towards the end of the book. The decision to quit will be purely yours, so don't be scared that you will have to quit in the end.

You may now think that in the end you will still continue smoking. All I can tell you at this moment is that it will not be that way. You have probably started smoking due to surroundings, friends, stress, influencers, or simply because you just wanted to see how it is. After a while, you got physically and mentally hooked up on it. Then, your mind probably started convincing you that you actually like doing this and you went on doing it, while it secretly feared the repercussions of quitting. If you really think that this is not the case and that you "really" enjoy smoking, then try to quit now, at least for a few days. You can't. Can you? No. Your mind will come up with hundreds of reasons for you to continue, and if one of them is because you actually like it, well, as I said, you are addicted. Just remember your first cigarette: was it that nice and pleasant? It wasn't, but your body adapted and made you like it due to the fear of quitting. But we will discuss this later. It's impossible to quit this way, uninformed, without going through withdrawal. It's natural. You don't really choose to smoke, as you cannot really choose to quit all of a sudden. Your body and mind request your daily and constant dose of nicotine. But this is not the real issue. This book is meant to make you understand what happens in your body at a biological and psychological level. This way you will better understand why you react the way you react to the impulse of smoking. You will see things with clear eyes and it will certainly be easier for you to quit.

Mainly, the fear of what happens after the first day of quitting is the thing that holds us down and does not allow us to quit or even consider quitting. You are afraid that you will not handle life's difficulties the way you are doing it now, and I'm talking here about daily pressures, stress, social activities and meetings and the fact that you will not be able to adapt to the new and improved lifestyle of a non-smoker. But the biggest fear of them is that once you are a non-smoker and you start enjoying your new life, you will have to admit that all those past years spent on smoking were ridiculous, wasted. You will have to admit that you made a mistake by throwing all that money away, that you intoxicated yourself so much and missed out so many things only because you simply continued this useless vice. Admit all these and move on. You are neither the first, nor the last person to have made mistakes. However, you can be one that wakes up, embraces reality and tries to fix the situation.

Warning!

This book does not contain medical advice. Before taking any measures, I recommend you to consult a doctor or a nutritionist.

THE BIOLOGICAL FACTOR

It is imperative for us to familiarize ourselves with the basic mechanisms of your body, so we can understand our potential for improvement. Once you will know how the body of a smoker works, why you get addicted to nicotine and how you will identify the measures that need to be taken against it, you will arrive faster at your desired result of being a non-smoker. We will not get into many biological details or do a complex study, but we will learn, in the easiest way possible, how the body works. In the next chapter, you will learn how the mind works in relation to smoking. Once you learn this information, it will be a lot easier to control and determine your mind to transform you into a non-smoker. You can sail the seas easier if you know which way the wind blows and how it affects your every movement.

We are inclined to fail when we address the problem of smoking only on a psychological level, leaving the biological factor aside. The truth is that it's necessary to focus on both, but for a strong mind we have to develop a strong body. The mind and the body are linked. They cooperate and if you want to make a change in your life, you need both the power of the mind and the power of the body.

WHY DO WE SMOKE?

At the beginning, we smoke out of curiosity or because we are pressed by various social influencers. Our friends smoke, we want to integrate ourselves into certain groups, we see others smoke and consider them "cool", mature and we want to be just like them. We also smoke because of the media: we are constantly assaulted with advertisements in which tough guys smoke on motorcycles, or after a fight, or love scenes in which the partners smoke, etc.. These factors, but not only them, influence us without even noticing it and after a certain period of time we want to try smoking, too. I will talk more about this in the psychological chapter called "why do we smoke".

So, we try our first cigarette. The taste is horrible. But we finish it because, most likely, there are other people next to us and we don't want to seem weak in their eyes. We don't actually like our first cigarette, we cough alarmingly, but at least we are not stigmatized. We now notice that we are in a trap from which we can escape very hard and we have laid the building blocks of a vice that will haunt us for a large part of our lives, destroying us, ruining us and slowing us down. At this point, we don't really understand what addiction is, but we will surely find out in a matter of time.

But why do we keep on smoking when nobody sees us, in situations where we don't have to show a false image of maturity? Maybe you have entirely forgotten by now why you actually started smoking. There is no human being that actually started smoking to get rid of stress or because they was bored and had nothing else to do. Everybody started smoking because they have been influenced in one way or another. At a certain point, we evolve and don't listen to people who try to convince us to smoke anymore. We can determine on our own that the ads are not how they seem. We realise that we were childish to deprive ourselves of health and money while we were releasing an unpleasant smell around us. We start realising these things and claiming that we will quit smoking. And, at first, we succeed in doing so, probably because of the money. But we can't actually quit for good. Now another question comes up: Why can't we?

WHY DO WE CONTINUE SMOKING?

There is no easy answer to this question. I mean there is, but it is too vague, and if we rely on that answer, we won't get too far. I will let you discover the complex answer to this question by yourself, in the next subchapters. The answer to this question can be found in each of the next subchapters, but it is not enough to simply mention it. We have to dig deeper into the information presented here. Learn about your enemy and you will be able to defeat him with his own tricks.

NICOTINE

Let's start with our worst and main enemy: Nicotine. It's a dangerous chemical. It's an odourless and oily substance that produces addiction. Compared to other drugs, it acts really fast. A small dose of nicotine is enough to get addicted – you will soon learn why. Nicotine is to be found in tobacco products, but nowadays, inventive, deceiving and profit-seeking companies have made it available in other forms too: nicotine patches, gum and electronic cigarettes.

After only 10 seconds of puffing, a small dose of nicotine is absorbed by your lungs through the millions of alveoli and then it travels to your brain through your blood. Thereafter, as long as you smoke, such a small dose is constantly released into your bloodstream. It's not a really big dose, but it's enough to cause all the torment you have been going through in all of these past years. Nicotine remains in your body for only a few hours. Its half-life is about 2 hours, after which it continuously decreases. Immediately after it has been completely eliminated from your body, you will start feeling its absence. Actually, it is not the absence of nicotine that causes withdrawal, but the psychological factor along with the biological factor makes us crave for cigarettes. Allow me to get into more detail.

When you are exposed to nicotine, the way your brain works literally changes. Imagine your brain as a computer that processes, stocks, and then uses information.

This information travels under the form of electricity through wires, just like our neurons which transfer and integrate information in our brain. Each neuron cooperates with thousands of other neurons. They contribute to information processing and make all the required adjustments before sending a message or a command to the body. The information travels through neurons in the form of electricity too, but it is, actually, submitted between neurons through a group of chemical messengers called neurotransmitters.

Each neurotransmitter has its own family of receptors. Nicotine copies the acetylene of the neurotransmitter and, thus, connects the receptors. Nicotine usually releases small quantities of acetylene in a regulated manner, but nicotine itself is not regulated by the organism. It activates cholinergic neurons (which, normally, would use the acetylene to establish connections with other neurons) in many regions of the brain. Due to the stimuli and the unregulated disruptions, the body releases more acetylene, determining a pronounced activity on the cholinergic paths of the brain. This determines your body and the brain to make you feel full of energy. The stimulation of the cholinergic neurons rises, also, the level of dopamine that activates the reward areas in our brain, released by the limbic system increases. When nicotine activates these paths, your wish to continuously use it occurs because you feel good due to the dopamine hormone.

When you inhale the first cigarette smoke, the nicotine determines the release of the hormone called epinephrine, which is usually released and activated when we are in a state of shock or scared. That hormone induces a state of extreme alertness so we can be more vigilant and be able to protect ourselves from possible threats. It also activates our nervous system, making breathing faster and superficial, giving us a false sense of energy. It sounds familiar, doesn't it? This hormone and the neurotransmitter are released through the adrenal gland. As you know, it accelerates the cardiac rhythm and the arterial pressure, while narrowing the blood vessels. Imagine how dangerous a cigarette actually is. You need the adrenaline only in dangerous situations with maximum risk only; for instance if you're being chased by a wolf. You receive the same amount of adrenaline when you smoke. Apparently, from a biological point of view, the body considers smoking as dangerous as a wolf ready to attack you.

Nicotine stimulates the production of dopamine, a neurotransmitter responsible for the area in our brain that provides us pleasure. I will talk about this substance in more detail in the next subchapter. Nicotine also stimulates the release of another neurotransmitter: glutamate, which is involved in learning, memorizing and enhances our neuronal connections. These stronger connections can constitute the physical base of our memory, and, due to nicotine, the glutamate creates a loop of sensations and pleasant memories which lead us to the desire of continuing to consume it. Nicotine also increases the levels of other neurotransmitters and chemical substances which determine the way our brain works. As a response to nicotine, the brain produces more endorphins, proteins that are natural painkillers. The chemical structure of endorphins is very similar to synthetic painkillers, such as morphine. They can create sensations of euphoria and can explain the psychoactive and fulfillers feeling of smoking.

Another harmful substance that is being inhaled along with the cigarette smoke, which also offers a relaxing and euphoric sensation, is carbon monoxide. Like nicotine, it enters the bloodstream through the lungs. Therefore, the oxygen level that is being transported by your red blood cells to your brain, heart and other organs decreases. The oxygen is being actually stopped by the carbon monoxide. The cells suffer a lack of oxygen and other nutrients due to the huge amount of carbon monoxide present. The cholesterol levels increase and it starts to deposit on the arterial walls, while in time, it thickens them. This fact causes heart diseases and heart attacks due to the rise in arterial blood pressure, cardiac rhythm and blood flow towards the heart.

Are you still following? Enough with the scientific part for now. It's frustrating especially when we don't understand most of these words, but we have to learn them. At driving school you also learn about things that you may think you will never use, but they are all part of the necessary knowledge a driver must have, in order to be able to drive informed and preventive. You too should be informed about the constant action and decision you are taking regarding smoking.

Nicotine remains in your organism for about seven to eight hours, but immediately after lighting up another cigarette you receive a new nicotine dose, and feel relaxed again due to the previously mentioned facts. Therefore, you delay your body's cleaning process and the stress inflicted onto the organism. Actually, from what you have learned so far, we deduce that while we smoke, our body functions like an over-revving engine. It works and still has power, but if you repeatedly over-rev the car, you wear it faster and, at a certain time, it breaks down.

Nicotine addiction happens instantly, from the first puffs. At the beginning, we don't like smoking, but we do it because of a few factors that influence us. After a while, we get used so much to the sensation of false relaxation induced by the cigarette that we believe it is actually caused by the cigarette itself, in a good way. We live under the impression of this false relaxation, but we do not realise that the cigarette actually caused the initial stress through the nicotine addiction, in a manner that we come to rely on it to sooth the damage it has provoked. After we go through the stage of not actually liking the cigarette, but we continue smoking, the body – through the various reactions mentioned earlier and through the aid of various neurotransmitters – will start to get stressed and ask us for more nicotine. The body will not be able to properly function anymore and it will stimulate our need for tobacco to improve our mood. Imagine how great we feel when we smoke a cigarette after we got stressed out. But I am pretty sure you have noticed by now that it's not the way it seems, the lack of nicotine itself has induced this mood upon you or has amplified a stressful mood you may have already experienced, alongside other external factors. When an external stress intervenes, the brain receives it, and because we have trained it well with tobacco, it knows that a cigarette will calm us down, but the real problem, the external factor that produced stress, isn't fixed yet. Due to the hormones released in your body, you may feel that you don't care about it anymore, thus seeming to ameliorate the situation and proving to your brain once more that cigarettes solve your problems. But they don't. You have entered a vicious, destructive cycle.

Once we try to become non-smokers, we inevitably confront ourselves with the outer stress and we chase away any thought that urges us to quit smoking. We live under the impression that cigarettes relax us and thus we are able to face stress much easier than a non-smoker, when actually it just masks our problems. Nicotine, in this case, is a small devil that hides in a corner and laughs at us when we self-deceive us and that seems to be stinging us with its pitchfork, urging us to continue feeding him while he gains more power over us.

The more you smoke, the more addicted you get to nicotine and so you will smoke even more in time to ensure the dose that the body is asking for. The body determines the release of dopamine and, by the abuse of this bodily function, the dopamine receptors start to get damaged. This way, we start to need a bigger dose of nicotine than before. This is why you may have noticed that a single cigarette will not satisfy you enough and you start lighting another one right after finishing the first one.

The more we fight to quit tobacco, the more addicted we get. The thought of us having to deal with stress without the soothing help of nicotine is another factor that makes us think with horror about quitting. Once nicotine is removed from the body, we will start feeling stress, so a cigarette will calm us down. If you don't smoke, you get stressed out of at least two reasons: the lack of nicotine and the actual external stress. Thus, having two fronts on which you have to fight, the chances of you lighting up a cigarette increase.

The tension caused by the treacherous nicotine makes us believe that we actually enjoy the taste and smell of cigarettes. Actually, we get immune to their disgusting taste. The smoke we inhale does not only burn our olfactory receptors and desensitizes them, but it also destroys our mouth's taste buds in such a manner that we cannot feel the unpleasantness of a cigarette anymore. Psychologically, the taste and smell of burning tobacco becomes acceptable. On the one hand, the mind fools us; on the other hand, the body fights the unpleasant smell and taste.

Now, maybe you are sceptic. You turn my words around, try to find excuses, justifications and probably claim you are not actually addicted. You consider the information presented to you in this chapter as fables or facts that apply only to weak people. You actually like smoking and can quit any time you want. You say you actually feel really good while smoking, you have no health problems and you don't get tired. These are nothing else but lies that we tell ourselves so that we don't feel "handcuffed" or "leashed", caught in a trap. We really don't like to admit we are subjects to something more powerful than ourselves. Yes, I admit, cigarettes might offer you energy due to the adrenaline, and yes, they might relax you, help you concentrate and calm you down. I don't deny it; I have actually admitted it in the previous pages. But this doesn't mean it does it in a healthy manner. If you would be a non-smoker, you would benefit from the same amount of energy and be able to naturally focus, yet nicotine overturns your entire hormonal system, causes an excessive adrenaline creation and wears your body out. This would not necessarily be a problem; you could continue smoking, but as a fact, you need your body, and leaving the waste of money aside, there are some other facts you should consider before lighting your next cigarette:

- Besides nicotine, tobacco contains other toxins as well, out of which 70 are known as carcinogenic and that easily enter the bloodstream, affecting other organs besides your lungs. I will not enter many details here, but I recommend you to inform regarding this danger. It's shocking how many diseases smoking can inflict.

- Smoking irritates your trachea, reduces lungs function and affects breathing. Because of these facts, you take less exercise, which leads to an unhealthy lifestyle and supports other harmful behaviours like alcoholism, procrastination, excessive eating etc.

- Smoking affects the immune system. You are more exposed to infections, and diseases like a simple common flu that can last longer. You have less antioxidants in your bloodstream, such as Vitamin C. A smoker has a constant lack of vitamin C.

- As a smoker, you are prone to periodontal diseases, diabetes, infertility, changes in physical appearance, such as premature aging.

Smokers live in average 10 years less than a non-smoker.

So far, I have not tried to convince you to quit smoking, but I have simply listed real facts on how the mind and body works and how they are negatively influenced. There is a lot more to learn, but it is important that we know all the data, that we understand it, and eventually use it against nicotine. The information presented here is scientifically proven, and denying it doesn't do you any good. It just increases your ignorance and makes your effort of becoming a non-smoker harder. Like it's certain that an antibiotic kills bacteria in your body, as obvious it is that nicotine creates addiction, whether you accept it or not.

DOPAMINE

Dopamine is a hormone and a neurotransmitter released by the brain into the body to reward you for the beneficial actions you have taken and successfully finished. It can also be launched before doing an action, to motivate you into doing it. This happens mostly if you have done the action before and you can anticipate pleasure, joy or victory before finishing the action. It adjusts our emotional mood and perception. It is involved in motivation, addiction, focus, desire and happiness. I will not get into details regarding its chemical and molecular structure, as these are not relevant for what I will try to exemplify.

As I previously stated, dopamine is a chemical substance that our brain releases and is responsible for motivation and focus. It also urges us to check our social accounts every time we get the chance – we necessarily must see the YouTube video that has suddenly appeared on our screen or check our recent notifications – but it also urges us to do useful stuff like eating and washing. It is literally responsible for motivation, that is, everything we do implies a small level of dopamine. Similarly, this hormone plays and important role in our survival and procreation. If you see food, dopamine gets released and you are motivated to eat. If you see attractive people, dopamine urges you to procreate. Without it, we would not function efficiently, and we would not achieve anything in life. Dopamine is released through olfactory and visual stimuli. You have already learned that while smoking, the body releases dopamine to thank you that you have rescued it from anxiety, which most likely was initially caused by the lack of nicotine itself. If you smoke too much and the concentration level of dopamine rises, its neuronal receptors get worn out. Dopamine has to be transported to the receptors so it can be efficient. If they are affected, then only a fraction of the released dopamine is transported and you will not feel its full stimulatory effects. You will light up cigarettes more often to receive the same amount of pleasure.

Thus, a simple, ordinary stimulation coming from other sources than tobacco isn't fulfilling because the dopamine receptors don't work properly. You will start to enjoy life less and less without cigarettes. In time, you will resort to other stimuli to receive your dopamine dose (alcohol, drugs, porn) while smoking more and more. Dopamine is the main cause for an addiction. There is however a solution to this issue: STOP SMOKING and let your receptors repair themselves naturally – I know; it is easier said than done.

As long as you affect your dopamine receptors with false stimuli that release dopamine, it will be even harder for you to carry out a beneficial activity, one that releases dopamine naturally, like sex, physical exercise or even getting your work done. Whereas the results of physical exercise cannot be seen immediately, the brain will not receive the stimulus, because of the worn out receptors, to motivate you into doing physical exercise and will rather determine you hold on to smoking. Moreover, your mind will start conceiving theories like "workout is not beneficial for you", "the effort is not worth it" and "you are happier smoking rather than engaging into useless physical activities". Now I am trying to convince you that if the receptors are affected and they are not able to absorb enough dopamine, it is imperative that you continue exercising other activities you know for sure they are beneficial, even if you do not receive the necessary stimuli to perform them. Once you are a non-smoker, you will have to head this way for a few days so you can offer those receptors time to heal.

The restoration process is fast if you stop intoxicating your body with nicotine and other false stimuli, and your life will turn to much better in no time.

Addiction is the hardest thing in life to fight. If you stop the regular release of dopamine caused by smoking, your brain will find no joy in any activity you are doing, at first. It won't have access to that source of joy anymore. However, dopamine is essential for the daily function of your brain. To repair the dopamine receptors in your neurons, you will have to persist in fighting against cigarettes. You may have lots of reasons to give up on your own way, but you have to fight the need for another cigarette if you want those receptors up and running again so you can start enjoying life. If you make improvements to your daily diet, the recovery speed will increase. Throw out unhealthy food and replace it with food rich in vitamins and nutrients, preferably vegetables that detoxify your body and reclaim your body's natural balance. Help your organism recover with cardiovascular stimulating exercise like swimming or jogging. We will carefully search these subjects in the following chapters, but for now I just want to draw your attention upon them. The more you expose your brain to unhealthy habits that abuse your dopamine production, the harder it will be for your receptors to heal. Think twice before engaging in such behavior; think about what you're giving up only so you can continue deceiving yourself into smoking.

If you would suddenly quit smoking, you would have to simultaneously confront the above mentioned problems alongside other. This is why it's better that you process all this new information and adapt it to your own lifestyle, slowly but progressively. And when the day comes and you quit for good, everything will flow very smoothly and you will start living better without you even noticing the change. You will ask yourself why did you even start smoking in the first place and why haven't you stopped sooner. Well, I'll tell you why: leaving modesty aside, you did need such a book to help you better understand what happens in your body while smoking and when quitting. You need all this information for that smooth transition into a life of a non-smoker; otherwise, withdrawal will likely be painful.

If you cannot convince yourself to do something, don't worry, dopamine levels can be increased. Not with medicine, but naturally. Once you learn how to control it, the receptors will repair, and, in the future, you'll be more easily motivated. To better understand what dopamine is and how it feels like, I will describe what feelings it stirs, so you will be able to identify it and generate with the force of your mind and positive thoughts. Imagine you have lots of money and meet a poor homeless person. You help that person buy food and they thank you with tearful eyes. The satisfaction feeling of helping somebody, the feeling you get when doing an unselfish deed is the feeling of dopamine.

Another example would be to imagine you have worked very hard on a project and, after months of efforts, you finally finished it. That feeling of completing something is caused by dopamine. Imagine a group of your co-workers starting to praise you, to appreciate the hard work you have done. The feeling of exaltation you experience is caused by dopamine. Its main function here is to reward you for a productive, finished task so you can go on and crave for another dopamine fix, through working more and improving your life. Now, you can see more clearly how dangerous for your life and goals it is to apply false dopamine fixes with cigarettes; in time you will not be able to do anything fulfilling.

Don't be fooled though by the other feature of dopamine that urges you to postpone work, tasks. Yes, dopamine can have a dark side, too, which is rather naturally innocent, but if we receive handouts, if other people do our work for ourselves, and we live a life where others serve us, we are prone to fall into this pit. Sometimes we feel that after a victory we deserve a little treat, a cigarette, unhealthy food or to simply laydown in bed and watch TV for the rest of the day, without doing anything else. It's alright for you to moderately eat and watch a movie, but don't fall into the trap of smoking cigarettes for the joy of finishing a big task. Once your dopamine receptors recover and you will be able to receive dopamine easier, from the simplest tasks like rearranging your desktop, you will be able to do many things that will improve your life, and all problems will seem to solve themselves on their own.

It would be ideal if we would not fall prey to any kind of addiction. The addicted brain cannot naturally distinguish between good and evil, right or wrong, and because of the subjugator, rotten and manipulative nicotine, it releases dopamine. If we light a cigarette, our brain will start producing dopamine to reward us. Because the lack of nicotine in a smoker's body will produce anxiety and stress, and the cigarette seems to relieve the smoker from those feelings, the brain will start believing that the cigarette is a "painkiller" and thus releases dopamine, to give us a state of wellbeing and encourage us to further smoke in such cases when we experience stress and anxiety. As a consequence, we smoke again and again to multiply the pleasant effects of dopamine. Then, we start getting addicted because we are offered a moment of satisfaction, although the lack of nicotine has caused our problems in the first place. If you study the result with intense care, you will notice that you don't actually get rid of the real problem. On the contrary, the dopamine that has been released due to cigarettes masks any kind of outer stress and you become "high", careless of it. Indeed, there is the possibility for dopamine to calm the outer stress, and thus you will be able to handle the causing-problem stress easier. As I said before, your body releases endorphins and adrenaline. But don't forget that it will do it with the constant threat of risking your health. Such stimuli can be found in engaging healthy activities, though. However, don't worry; in a future chapter we will analyse what other activities can be triggered by this hormone in a healthy way, so you may be able to improve your life not only by becoming a non-smoker, but by obtaining dopamine through other productive sources rather than tobacco.

Let's recap:

- Dopamine is a hormone that is released by the brain. It gives you a feeling of wellbeing, of thankfulness, joy, whenever you do something beneficial for your body. It motivates you to eat or work.

- Because nicotine, through its structure, can cause addiction, the lack of it causes the body to experience stress.

- When you smoke, you receive nicotine, the stress diminishes and adrenaline and endorphins are released.

- Your mind associates the decrease of stress with cigarettes. It thanks you, offering you dopamine. It starts to believe that smoking actually helps you, and it starts encouraging you to continue smoking in other stressful situations as well, whether they are caused by nicotine, or external factors. Your mind will actually start to beg you to smoke, and not only when you lack nicotine...

Now that you understand, at least superficially, how dopamine works and how the brain releases it into your system as a "thank you" method for calming your nicotine-caused stress, you can apply this new information to techniques in fighting nicotine and other vice-causing substances like sugar, alcohol but also to addictive behaviour like gambling. In the future, we will turn dopamine against smoking, in such a manner that you will receive it as a reward only if you do NOT smoke. Currently, nicotine has tricked your mind in believing that smoking makes you feel good, but you will trick it back in receiving dopamine from non-destructive behaviours. Actually, this is the way it all works naturally. Currently, your receptors are worn out, damaged, so we will have to approach unusual methods until we will be able to fix the problem. For this, we first had to study and better understand the mechanism and the way in which dopamine is released.

WITHDRAWAL

When nicotine is introduced into the body for a long period of time, the neurotransmitters balance is disturbed. We suddenly take the decision to be non-smokers and feel the secondary, physical and psychological effects caused by the abstinence from nicotine, like hunger cravings and mood-swings.

We experience withdrawal every time we are deprived of nicotine for a long period of time. And we don't like this feeling at all. We continue smoking because we are afraid of intensifying the withdrawal that could run out of control and disable us carrying out our daily tasks. The withdrawal symptoms are worse in the first 2-3 days, softening in the next 3-4 weeks. In this period, our body removes nicotine. The physical symptoms last only a few days actually, until the entire nicotine leaves our body, until the dopamine receptors rebuild and start functioning properly and until our body adapts to the new healthy lifestyle. The psychological part of withdrawal can last longer, according to how well we prepare for it.

Yet it is surely unpleasant to experience withdrawal, but don't worry, it is not permanent. A withdrawal episode usually lasts about 10 minutes. When you become a non-smoker, every time you successfully go through withdrawal, you are getting closer to not experiencing it at all. After each episode passes, it gets weaker and weaker. There is no evidence found or even speculated about the dangers of withdrawal to one's body.

Paul Bernard Gaspar

In order for you to better understand withdrawal and how it feels like to quit smoking, I will use an allegory. Imagine you have to climb a mountain. At the beginning, you climb it easily and full of energy, with a lot of enthusiasm and ambition. Nonetheless, as you progress, you feel like you are not making any progress. Climbing starts feeling harder and harder. You get very tired and you start asking yourself why you are doing this in the first place when you could have nicely stayed at home in your comfy bed. At a certain time, if you don't give up, you are able to see the mountain's peak, which is still far away, and you are still very tired. Wouldn't it be a shame to quit right in that moment? The more you get closer to the peak, the more exhausted you are, but, paradoxically, you seem more energetic and your mind encourages you: "Come on, don't give up, there's just a bit more to climb, the hardest part is over." You finally reach the top and it seems like all your tiredness is gone. Small tip: endorphins and dopamine for completing this exhausting task. That's the way resisting withdrawal and quitting cigarettes for good will feel like. Until you reach the peak you may have to struggle a bit and force your inner thoughts of giving up, but simply remind yourself how far you made it and how close you are to succeed. It's not impossible, rather if you resist long enough and fight off any negative thought of quitting, you WILL eventually arrive at the "peak" and you will gloriously look down to your own past, to the road that brought you there. You will forget how hard

45

it was, or at least you will leave those thoughts aside and embrace the glory of victory.

We hear everywhere about the terrible withdrawal symptoms and the pain it is associated with, the torment you have to go through because of it. It's really discouraging. Once you want to quit and feel the slightest crumb of withdrawal, you surrender due to the exaggerations you may have heard and imagine and your mind starts building up fictional stories of how hard it will be for you. You may think you will be unable to get some sleep, a good night's rest. We all have nights in which we cannot sleep well. If you lose a few hours of sleep in the initial phase, don't worry; your gain after you do succeed is much greater. You may be probably thinking that you will wake up tired after you finally do fall asleep, but your oxygenated blood and reinvigorated body, due to the absence of nicotine and the other toxins within a cigarette, will compensate for that tiredness. Do not blame withdrawal! Maybe you ought to blame your own lifestyle if you really don't sleep well. Are you keeping track of how much coffee, caffeine-rich drinks or other natural stimulates you ingest? Well, you should. When quitting for good, you will receive lots of natural energy, so you will not need these synthetic incentives anymore. Worst case scenario, you can take sleeping pills until your body adapts to the new, healthier lifestyle.

Withdrawal is as biologic as it is psychological. In the chapters I discussed about nicotine and dopamine, you have learned how it biologically manifests. Once your body starts to remove the toxins in your body, especially the nicotine, you offer it the possibility to recover and restore its dopamine receptors and you start gaining the dopamine from other productive and healthy sources of pleasure. Withdrawal at that point should no longer concern you. It doesn't really last as long as it may seem, especially if you respect your body's biological needs and help it recover. The following chapters will enlighten you further and help you fulfil these needs. Maybe you will not even feel any withdrawal this way, and if you do feel the slightest symptom, you will get over it with great ease. You are getting stronger and stronger with each word you read.

The psychological withdrawal is the hardest to overcome. You can fight it only if you change your attitude towards smoking and only if you really want to become a non-smoker. Let's suppose that, for now, you don't want to quit. It's not a big problem. But maybe your subconscious does want it for you. If you take the steady decision to improve your life by quitting smoking, accept that it is possible, but not compulsory, to have serious withdrawal symptoms and embrace the fact that they pass after just a few hours or days, then you will get over the psychological withdrawal very easily. You'll see, your own mind and its fears is what is actually preventing you from even trying to quit. As long as you are able to learn to embrace those fears, knowing that it is possible to quit and that through the information you are learning, fighting withdrawal will actually feel like a challenge. It'll be like something you are eager to do, to try out and prove to everybody that you can do it.

You don't have to be afraid of quitting; you don't have to be afraid of a bad, hard withdrawal. It's not like you have to cut off your own finger. You are not damaging yourself. If you live under the impression that you could not resist the lack of pleasure induced by tobacco, you will not succeed. You will have to convince yourself that you are not quitting on pleasure; rather you are simply quitting a destructive vice, which you will replace with a long, healthy, dynamic and happy life together with your loved ones.

I must warn you: it is possible to suffer from the following psychological withdrawal symptoms, but they can be improved if you understand what exactly is causing them, if you accept them as such and you realise that they pass and will remain only a disposable memory:

- The intense desire to smoke. You end up constantly thinking about cigarettes. But I guarantee you that this does not last for more than 30 minutes, even less, if you manage to find yourself other distractions;

- Irritability and frustration. This is normal, you don't get what you want, and you get frustrated, but you should use reverse psychology and turn your feelings against it. Cigarettes. Why should you be angry on yourself and on the fact that you are not allowed to destroy your body, when you can be angry on the cigarettes that have caused you feel this way? Actually, if you think about it, withdrawal is caused by the cigarettes that you need so bad, so you should start hating them rather yourself or those around you. If you manage to do this, you will notice that you simply no longer want to smoke. Just convince your subconscious that your anger is wrongly oriented;

- Bad mood. You surely experienced bad mood while you were smoking too, now you can endure some extra days feeling this way without cigarettes, considering how much you will gain after that. You will seek conflicts only so you will be able to run/hide away and smoke. If you notice your behaviour resembles to what I have described above, remember that the fault lies in nicotine, especially in the lack of it. Do you really want to offer it even more power over yourself by obeying to it and feeding yourself with another dose?

- Difficulty focusing. Of course you are unable to focus on anything if all you can think of are cigarettes. Don't try, just do it; meditate, pull yourself together. Lack of focus isn't a reason so you can continue destroying your life or even your future if you think about it;

- Anxiety. Personally, I suffered from anxiety in my early withdrawal stage, but it has been caused by the last cigarette I had, without me even realizing it. Only after further study have I learned that smoking releases the hormone called cortisol as a stress response, inducing a state of alertness. Because there isn't any real danger around us, the hormones' role is keeping us alert in case of danger; we tend to focus on negative aspects of our lives because of this hormone, which may result into anxiety.

After all, you have to accept that these symptoms exist. There is nothing you can do; you have to go through them. But how much they affect you and their intensity is entirely up to you, on how open you are to the information I am presenting you and the measures you will take to improve them. Think about what your final gains will be. You'll see! If it would have been so easy to quit, you may have done it already in the past; you and millions of other people.

For some, the crave for cigarettes lasts longer, for others less. In average, it lasts for about 10 to 15 minutes. The moment you feel it, you should distract yourself from it through various ways or tasks. As this crave is predominantly psychological, it's enough for you to watch a funny or educational video whilst experiencing it, so that you overcome it.

Some places and activities trigger the desire to smoke, for instance, talking on the phone, stress, caffeine intake and alcohol consumption, boredom, or, obviously, the presence of other smokers. The idea is to avoid all of these triggers in the first days, so you won't experience the desire to smoke too often. This may be really frustrating and could divert you from your goal. The desire to smoke generally appears only when you confront such a trigger, and mostly only when you remember that you haven't smoked for a while. Then, it will manifest in physical feelings. I will get into more details about how to fight crave for smoking in a future chapter. Until then, you should learn about further triggers and biological and psychological phenomena that occur in your body both while you smoke and after you become a non-smoker.

CAFFEINE

Before you get sceptic and I start losing your attention due to this highly sensitive chapter, please understand that I won't ask you to stop drinking coffee. I don't want you to think that quitting smoking means to quit other small joys in life, but it is important for you to understand that, at least in your first days as a non-smoker, coffee won't help you very much. I will explain why and how you can continue drinking it without any temptation to smoke. Turning into a non-smoker is rather a psychological process, than a biological one, but it is directly correlated to the latter and to the phenomena that automatically occur in your body. That is why, we focus now on the biological factor of quitting, which you will be able to understand, master and use to influence your psyche, as I will show you in the hypoglycemia chapter.

Most smokers drink coffee. They are actually excited to combine cigarettes with coffee. It feels like one without the other is like a hotdog without mustard; it doesn't make any sense. There is no pleasure in drinking coffee without a cigarette, especially in the morning. The first cigarette that a smoker lights up in the morning next to his coffee mug is like a sacred ritual. It makes us feel better, it wakes us up. Cigarettes offer us adrenaline, coffee offers us caffeine; this way, our mornings are filled with happiness. As a smoker, you know well that there are no moments in which you can find greater joy in a cigarette than when you also drink coffee. However, this is exactly the problem. Just like you need a cigarette next to your morning coffee, so it will feel when you will be a non-smoker.

This issue can crush you down in your first days of abstinence. You used to smoke while drinking coffee, you actually made a habit out of it, and your mind has been taught to combine them both, like it knows to combine toothpaste to a toothbrush. That is why, it would be best for you to give up coffee for a few days only, so you aren't tempted to smoke or so you aren't tormented by the absence of a cigarette from your routine. Do this at least during the first days, until the hardest part of the withdrawal disappears. It will be much easier for you to remove this important smoking trigger.

I know: you need the energy that is being provided by coffee so you can face your daily tasks. Maybe you will get dizzy, maybe you will get tired without coffee. To make it even worse, withdrawal will pull you down, too. To handle this situation, you can replace the energy you would get from coffee through other natural incentives like green coffee, black tea or detoxifying tea. A smoker always lacks vitamin C, so you can add some lemons to your tea. Add honey for the glucose as well; it will revive your spirit and energy and you will not perceive the process of quitting as being tiresome.

If you really can't hold on without coffee, if you work a lot and you simply cannot afford to risk your job because of the physical distress and lack of focus, then you can have it. But do it quickly. Don't hold on to it for hours, because your mind will tease you to light a cigarette. Believe me, your mind will find a lot of reasons for you to smoke during this. It will try to convince you that one cigarette won't do any harm. Can it? Well, it can. As you have learned so far, it's enough for just a few puffs to get you addicted again, especially if you are already used to smoking. Rinse your mouth after you drink coffee so you won't feel the taste for the next hours. Even if you will be busy and might not notice the coffee taste in your mouth, your subconscious surely will feel it and it will start bugging you into smoking, without you even realising why.

Usually, smokers drink more coffee per day than a non-smoker for a certain reasons. The chemical breakdown of nicotine lasts about three days from your last cigarette. This process has an impact on caffeine, because, in the presence of nicotine, the chemical breakdown of coffee is twice as fast. In other words, the refreshing effect of coffee disappears faster. We get to drink more coffee to obtain the same dose of energy and we slowly become immune to it and its effects, just like in the case of dopamine. In the first days after quitting smoking, when you still have a small amount of nicotine in your bloodstream, your glycaemia collapses, you get tired, you get angry and irritated, and you start drinking coffee to fight the lack of energy produced by the withdrawal agony. But coffee has no more effect upon yourself, so you are even more irritated, hostile and cranky. At first, it would be best to stop drinking coffee, until you become receptive to it again, so that when the time comes for you to become a non-smoker you won't have to face and fight a lack of vitality. If nicotine has tricks to make you continue smoking, then there are tricks to stop smoking too and to be more dynamic, to feel well, even better actually.

ALCOHOL

As a smoker – as you already know – alcohol stirs the need to smoke, too. You barely feel it on the tip of your tongue and it already requests for a smoke. I strongly recommend you to avoid it in the first weeks, so you won't torture yourself and won't give in. Drinking coffee keeps you aware so that you can fight withdrawal, but if you drink alcohol, you might lose control and give in.

Alcohol is a depressive agent that can exaggerate any feelings. It's normal to be sad sometimes. Emotions are the salt and pepper in our lives. Emotions make you feel alive, human. But we don't have to put too much "salt" on our issues; I mean we don't have to worsen emotional moods with alcohol, especially not in this period of time when you might be in your most vulnerable point due to withdrawal and its collateral effects. Alcohol will not make you think clearly, so if you will have to face a problem, you won't find a solution to it. On the contrary, its consequences will be even worse. Alcohol suppresses positive thoughts. When you wake up from drunkenness, you remain with the negative feelings and you don't have any solutions to your problems. So, what I mean is, if you drink out of misery and sorrow, you do it in vain.

Your problems still persist whether you face them sober or drunk, but what's worse, if you drink, you focus mainly on the negative aspects of the problem, disabling yourself to find a solution. Thus, you will find yourself surrounded by anxiety, which will in turn awake your desire to smoke.

Generally, I argue it's preferably you don't drink alcohol. It's not healthy, it helps you gain weight due to its chemical composition and you waste money in building up a possible future vice. But this is another topic. If you suffer from alcoholism, you can replace the words "cigarette" and "nicotine" in almost any part of this book with "alcohol" and you will succeed in quitting excessive drinking, too. But let's focus for now on the most dangerous vice, nicotine, respectively smoking.

DEHYDRATION

Smokers are constantly dehydrated from various reasons. One of these is the fact that they inhale a lot of hot smoke and exhale moist and warm smoke. Also, their bodies are in a permanent process of natural detoxification. The body alarms itself because of the huge quantity of toxins inside of it and it begins to eliminate them through different ways. The urinary flow increases especially when you are consuming more coffee than usual, because coffee is a diuretic. Due to the fact that smokers consume more caffeine-rich drinks, they consume less water, but eliminate more, they tend to be constantly dehydrated.

Even if you have dehydration symptoms, such as the lack of energy or tiredness, they can be masked through the stimulatory effects of nicotine, but also by the cortisol and adrenaline. So, when the glycaemia levels rise, the quantity of stress hormones rise, too. It is a sensation of false energy that compensates for thirst and dehydration caused by cigarettes. What I am trying to point out is that when you quit smoking and you manage to control your caffeine intake, hypoglycemia and dehydration, you might not experience any withdrawal at all. How is this possible? You avoid skipping meals to maintain your blood sugar at optimal levels. If you cannot eat a substantial meal, try at least having a nutrition bar with you. Eat breakfast so you can maintain a stable blood sugar and drink a lot of water.

You will notice that these biological symptoms will create irritability and tiredness, and your mind will mistake them with the lack of nicotine, thus making you smoke once again. It is believed that cigarettes actually offer you energy, when you actually just put your body in a position of extreme alertness and stress while smoking, and, in order to fight symptoms, it will give you artificially-induced energy. This is slowly wearing your body out instead of getting the same amount of energy from natural sources. If you would manage to respect your body's biological needs, as a non-smoker naturally and unconsciously does, you would experience a far better life than the one you currently have.

Don't forget to drink lots of lemon water. A smoker is constantly deprived of vitamin C, which, besides being an excellent antioxidant, it naturally fills you with energy. Lemon water helps maintain the health of the digestive system and metabolic rate while maintaining a balance between your body's minerals, which you could lose through sweat while exercising, or when the body uses them to eliminate nicotine and other harmful toxins.

If you manage to replace any drink with simple water, lemon water or various teas, you will have the following benefits:

- You lose weight faster. For instance, if you constantly drink only water for a few days instead of any kind of juices or sodas, you will lose as many calories as you would normally do by running 5 miles.
- You accelerate your metabolism while obtaining more vitality.
- You control your cravings easier; you don't feel withdrawal and you won't have the excuse to blame your lack of smoking for any bad mood.
- Your brain functions way better. You keep it hydrated, which is natural.
- The body excretes toxins faster;
- The heart, which needs a lot of water, will function better.

HYPOGLICEMIA / LOW BLOOD SUGAR

How is this possible? Surprisingly enough, low blood sugar is a reason that makes you continue smoking. It doesn't seem to have any apparent connection to it, but if you keep on reading, you will realise that it actually does. Cigarettes repress our appetite. Therefore, we may sometimes be tempted to skip eating, especially breakfast. Instead, we drink coffee and smoke a few cigarettes before heading off to work. While we are smoking, the body produces adrenaline. This determines an increase in blood sugar level together with an increase in fat, thus creating an illusion of vitality. Now you can notice too that what cigarettes seem to offer is actually the body's response to further stress. When you remove cigarettes and you don't give the body enough "fuel" –food, especially breakfast – then the blood sugar drops. What are the symptoms of this drop you may ask? Irritability, lack of focus, restlessness. Once again we have unmasked a smoking myth. It is not the fact that we don't smoke which creates this restlessness, but, among others, a low blood sugar, that can be easily brought to normal levels by simply eating. Low blood sugar can make you experience a painful withdrawal. Keep this in mind when you will quit smoking for good, and, spoiler alert, you will. You will have to eat regularly to keep your blood sugar at optimal levels, to fight any withdrawal symptoms. Don't be scared, you will not gain weight; at least not as long as you take care on how much you eat.

THE METABOLISM

A short definition: "The metabolism is the physical and chemical process that generates energy in a cell or in an organism. The transformation of food in the body is a function of the metabolism. The metabolic rate describes how fast these processes occur."

Lots of people postpone the day to quit smoking for good because they are afraid they will gain weight. I admit that I have postponed it myself, from various related reasons: either I was single and did not want to gain weight so I could find someone, so I won't be less attractive, or an important event was coming up and I wanted to look well and fit into my clothes.

You have to know that the possibility of weight gain does exist when you stop smoking. However, don't discourage yourself. It all depends on you and how you manage the situation. Now that you have this book in your hands and you can inform yourself on the entire process of quitting smoking, you have huge chances of maintaining your weight. Worst case scenario, if you do gain weight, it will be a minimal amount that you will lose in a few weeks.

Your metabolism changes when you quit smoking.

Your appetite returns, your taste buds regenerate and your sense of smell improve. This issue will also be fixed, don't worry. Not everybody gains weight, at least not as much as they admit. Most of the people that do gain weight owe it to the fact that they simple eat more, uncontrollably. The first step in maintaining your weight would be to have a balanced diet which means nothing more than you used to eat before.

After you quit smoking, your body will ask you to continue. It will generate a sensation of hunger. You might confuse nicotine craving with hunger and so you will start eating more, to fill that void. Therefore, you don't gain weight because of quitting smoking *per se*, but because you want to soothe the "hunger" sensation left by the lack of nicotine. You might end up drinking more alcohol to suppress that feeling; watch out! Besides, you will create a new vice, the temptation to smoke will be amplified and you might become subjugated to smoking. Plus, the alcohol itself will make you gain weight.

Once you get through the first days of withdrawal, you strengthen your willpower and discipline and thus you will be able to control your diet, too. You will become stronger from this point of view and you will improve this aspect of your life as well. Behold a big advantage a new non-smoker holds: he/she is more careful to details and realises the fact that his/her diet isn't healthy, and may be able to take measures in this aspect.

Smoking increases your metabolic rate because it forces the heart to beat faster. Each cigarette contributes to the increase of each beat per minute. If you smoke all day, you will have a constant high blood pressure and your pulse will increase. This fact causes continuous stress on the heart and plays an important role in heart diseases. When you become a non-smoker, both the cardiac rhythm and the metabolic rate decrease. This change, along with the diet changes (due to the fact that you regain your sense of smell and your taste buds regenerate) can lead to gaining extra pounds. Now that you understand why you might be able to gain extra weight, you can realize that it is possible to maintain your weight by simply respecting your body's rules and the way it works. You can simply increase your metabolic rate, which is healthy overall.

Physical exercise burns calories and stimulates the metabolism up to 24 hours after ending any exercise. Nicotine triggers dopamine release, the neurotransmitter responsible for the sensations of pleasure and joy. Once you stop smoking, its receptors start to heal; the brain will not release dopamine more easily after you eat and it will amplify the temptation to eat more often. Exercise releases the same hormone in a more efficient manner, without endangering our health and without helping us gain weight; it rather helps us loose or maintain it. In the end, it doesn't really matter if you eat more, you may do so, but compensate with more physical exercise to stimulate your metabolism and burn calories. Exercise decomposes fat and releases it into the bloodstream so that your body may use it for energy. This way you will be able to diminish your hunger.

Any kind of physical exercise matters when you want to support your metabolism and fight any effects that may lead to weight gain after quitting. As a bonus for the effort, your overall health and energy increase. In another chapter, I will discuss about exercise and I will suggest what kind of activities you can do to support your metabolism, maintain your weight or even loose a few pounds. I currently recommend you to start stretching, doing yoga, riding a bicycle, sprinting or even swimming from time to time so you can warm up for your future, improved, lifestyle.

Even if you gain extra weight while starting to adapt to your new life as a non-smoker, you can stop it by being careful at what you're doing. Relax, gaining extra weight doesn't go on forever; you may add just a few pounds in the first weeks. After that, your metabolism will adjust and, at a certain point, will properly function, as it did before when you used to smoke. If you do physical exercise, you even might not suffer any visible change.

Statistics show that you can add up to six pounds in the year after quitting smoking. The subjects that took part in these statistics did not have the occasion to read this book, haven't eaten healthier and haven't adjusted their diet.

Honestly, this isn't bad at all considering all your other "gains" in life after quitting. For most people, weight starts to automatically decrease after this period, after the metabolism readjusts. In the end, gaining weight is prone to happen because we try to substitute the act of smoking by eating more after we quit. We may recover, but this isn't as dramatic as it seems. The best approach in case you do gain extra weight isn't controlling your weight, but focusing on strategies meant to keep you healthy.

Maybe I started to be as annoying as a social network ad, or one of those website popups, but allow me to recommend you a mixture I have been consuming and that had surprising effects over my health and metabolism: ginger with honey and lemon. The diuretic effect of lemons helps eliminating toxins inside the body and excess water, burns fat and raises the metabolic rate. The ginger improves your digestive functions, activates the metabolism and helps detox your body. Honey may be added to this mixture for flavour, but also for the energy it provides. These ingredients also strengthen your immune system and bring many benefits during your withdrawal period: increased focus, reduced dizziness, regulated blood sugar and revived body. You can find various recipes on the Internet to prepare this mixture.

Before you start a new diet, perform physical exercise (especially if you aren't usually very active), or even try the above mentioned mixture, I recommend you to consult a doctor.

We are all different, we react differently to various sorts of food, and that is why it's for the best you consult at least a licensed nutritionist concerning your diet.

DIET

So far, maybe you started to feel a deep ambition inside knowing that you will get to save money and live a healthier life due to the improved lifestyle, but it is important to start with realistic goals. First, don't think that everything will happen at once, especially regarding your lifestyle. That is why I recommend you not to make any sudden changes, rather progressive ones. Focus on one change at a time, until you adapt it to your lifestyle, then move on to the next goal. Otherwise, you will feel motivated at first and full of energy, but be careful – if you propose too many changes at once in your life, you risk failing and relapsing to your previous lifestyle, and eventually to smoking. The fight with nicotine is pretty hard itself alone, you don't need to "attack" multiple fronts at once. Some minor adjustments in your diet and lifestyle should be enough at first. You don't have to start eating only salads; just simply add them to your diet while replacing something else, like bread. Instead of junk food, eat homemade popcorn; they have fewer calories and keep you nourished for a long period of time. Try eating carrots as snacks, nuts or unroasted peanuts. If you start a new diet at the same time with quitting smoking, it might be too hard. This is why I recommend you to include these healthy items into your diet once at a time, starting now. At the end of the book, I will tell you about the 7 days I used to prepare for quitting, how I physically and mentally prepared for the process, and in those chapters I will also talk more about how I changed my own diet.

If you can hold a diet during your withdrawal phase, I congratulate you and I encourage you to do so, but if you feel like you are losing patience and control, just go back to your normal eating habits. Eventually, leave room for some healthy snacks. Don't forget the main goal: quitting. Then, you can focus on any other improvements. It's more important to fight nicotine and its withdrawal symptoms at first, while trying to take care of your metabolic changes, but don't try quitting and eating healthier if you can't simply handle both of them. I'm realistic, although lots of other authors claim that you can do miracles. You could, but nobody knows your lifestyle and your already set up routine. Only you know how to handle these changes. If you do add a few extra pounds, it's ok. Carefully, you won't add much at all, maybe one or two, but those will not affect you too much and you can lose them after your withdrawal phase.

You have to be very careful. Food can turn into a substitute for smoking, especially because quitting makes you feel like something is missing.

In the absence of cigarettes, you may feel like you don't know what to do with your hands; the subconscious turns rather nostalgic for your hand-to-mouth action you used to do with cigarettes, so it will start replacing that action with hand-to-mouth actions, such as eating. Everything will taste better due to the regeneration of your taste buds that will no longer be blocked by tar. But simply because the food will start tasting better, there is no reason for you to start eating more. You can't stop eating as easily as you stopped smoking, but only you can take the decision of not gaining extra weight. Simply don't eat more than you used to and do some extra exercise to maintain your metabolic rate that you had when you used to smoke. Any kind of extra exercise is a win.

When you start confusing nicotine cravings with food appetite, simply watch out at how much you are eating. If you notice that you are eating more than before, you probably fell into the nicotine's trap, but you can easily escape this by reducing your meals size. In case you do add those extra pounds in the first weeks, keep calm. Don't get tempted to start smoking again only because you might think that it will help you lose the extra weight. It doesn't work this way. You won't. You simply will be maintaining the extra weight you gained. Anyway, once you become a non-smoker, you will feel more dynamic, your self-confidence will increase and you will be able to lose weight easily. All in all, it's more important to quit smoking than adding a few extra pounds which you can deal with later.

Spoiler alert: I managed to quit smoking and I haven't added any weight because I had the willpower and energy, due to my positive thinking, to control my diet and overall health. Thus, I managed to adjust other aspects of my life as well, harder ones. Gradually, I succeeded, and you can succeed too!

Here are some ideas that you can apply at this point. Even if you don't reach your dietary goal, you can still improve your eating habits and your situation:

- Watch out for your meals size. You don't have to eat a lot at once, but less and more often, so you can be able to maintain your blood sugar at optimal levels. Try eating nutritious and healthy food. Don't eat any junk food only for the love of it;

- Read the product labels when buying your groceries. Find out what they contain. Don't consume fatty products or foods rich in calories;

- Beware of temptations. Don't fill your place with junk food; instead choose a diet based on nutritive substances, like nuts. If it is hard for you to do so, ask your family to help you during this period. Ask them to cook healthier food until you get used to the transition;

- You can eat sweets and ice-cream, but as I said,

don't fill your home with them. Don't have them handy when you have nicotine cravings, otherwise you will eat them without further thought and will risk adding extra weight. Simply treat yourself when you are outdoors. Healthy replacements for sweets and their cravings are fruits.

- Drink a lot of water. If you feel like eating a snack, drink a glass of water before eating anything. Maybe add a slice of lemon to it, just for the taste. Your appetite will alleviate because the lemon will give you a sense of satiety. Also, constant hydration lowers nicotine cravings;

- Distract yourself with other activities when junk food cravings appear. Aim to eat small quantities only after you finish your housework or exercise.

SLEEP

All the talk about the metabolism and diets are useless if we don't get enough sleep. Lack of sleep can cause the body to accumulate fat, so it may be able to offer you energy during the day. This means you will gain weight.

You might not be able to sleep more than you already do, and your sleep might not be enough.

You may have lots of work to do, your children keep you up at night, the neighbor's dog is barking. Don't alarm yourself and don't get discouraged. Think about the things you can do to offer yourself a better, restful sleep and take gradual measures to improve it.

People that are very busy tend to reduce the amount of sleep they have so that they can finish their daily housework. However, if you reduce your sleep time, you will be more tired, you will work slower and without energy. So, if you would sleep a bit more, you would surely get more things done with the extra energy.

Lack of sleep may affect your productivity, creativity, focus, patience and might cause anxiety – things we should avoid while trying to quit smoking. Actually, maybe you have noticed, the symptoms of sleep deprivation resemble to withdrawal symptoms, and you might confuse them, tempting you to give up quitting so you can return to your normal, productive lifestyle. Less sleep means a less efficient body, which, overall, means a less healthy body. Anything you seem to be doing isn't gathering the desired results. The role of this chapter is for you to understand that if you do manage to sleep more, you can achieve far more things than by working in the hours you have cut off your sleep. Don't live under the impression that you are wasting time sleeping, rather think about the moments you were most productive: when you were exhausted, or rather when you were well rested?

Lack of sleep slows down our brains functions. We tend to react slower, and in many critical situations, wrongly, like in the decision of quitting. It has been scientifically proven that lack of sleep lowers neuronal activity from the prefrontal cortex. This region is associated with planning, decision making, problem solving, focus and reasoning. That's why you are dizzy when you wake up too early or when you don't sleep enough. When being sleep deprived, it's harder for you to finish a thought, to be creative or to face difficulties. In the case of a smoker, the subconscious will assume any command, whilst ignoring the conscious mind, and it will act upon its primary instincts and build-in, standard thoughts that it has stored in so far. This means, when you are sleep deprived, you can't think straight, clearly, and you might refer to your basic instinct of smoking, while actually forgetting your goal.

Sleep deprivation can affect your personality, too. The prefrontal cortex shows less activity when you don't sleep enough. The amygdala, the area in your brain associated with information processing on an emotional level, is more active when you are sleep deprived. So, if you sleep less, the responses of your brain to negative stimuli are more intense. The less you sleep, the more you interpret situations in a negative manner, you tend to exaggerate and you have a worse mood than usual. When quitting smoking, it would be best if you could maintain yourself rested at least for a period of time. You don't want to lose control over your mind and body and fall in nicotine's trap once again only because you cut off an hour of sleep.

The brain isn't the only thing that needs sleep, but also the metabolism. If you don't sleep enough, the Ghrelin hormone levels start rising. This determines the accumulation of fat in the body and causes a feeling of hunger. A single sleepless night can cause a raise of 15% of this hormones level inside the body. In other words, if you sleep less, you will experience more hunger and you will probably end up eating more, especially because you can't think clear.

The stress-inducing hormone, namely cortisol, also starts rising its levels if you don't rest enough. This may raise the level of visceral fat, the fat which stays the longest inside our body and the one we fight the most.

Nowadays we live busy lives. Most people probably don't get enough sleep. But if we manage to understand that, once we get enough rest, we can work with greater vigor and even more, we save time by doing so, we eat less which means we don't accumulate visceral fat (and don't blame ourselves for being fat), then we would grant sleep more importance. Even one extra hour of sleep can bring you 2 to 3 extra hours per day of efficient work, especially if you add up all the benefits you get through rest.

THE ILLUSION OF HEALTH

Another factor that determines us to continue smoking is the illusion of being healthy: we smoked so far and we are fine, we feel well, there is no sign that smoking affects us. The illusion of health currently fogs our perception and makes us believe that everything will turn out to be fine even if we continue smoking. Smokers know the risks tobacco implies, so there is no reason to list them all because you wouldn't have the patience and willpower to go through all of these pages. But smokers stop there. They admit they are aware of some health risks, but they do not understand them for sure. You too, as a smoker, if you truly understand these real risks, you would certainly quit smoking right now. It would be impossible for you not to do so. Smoking brings no real benefits, and if you could actually see what happens to your body because of it, the faster you would quit. But you can't see, and you tend to ignore the cases that are broadcasted online or on TV, those disturbing images of smoking diseases. It's like the subconscious tries to prevent us from seeing and acknowledging them, while trying to prevent us from the negative feelings we might experience while seeing them. It starts to mask them, or make you consider them exceptions that couldn't possibly happen to you. Our brain lies to us and we are truly unaware of the risks smoking brings.

Maybe you cough without giving it any attention.

As a smoker, you tend to cough more often than a non-smoker. This kind of cough is a clear sign that the body tries to eliminate the toxic substances that have been inhaled. Coughing is the natural process of the body to remove foreign substances from the lungs, such as: water, tar and various toxins. Smokers avoid physical exercise because they feel tired all the time and breathe heavily because of the cigarettes and the tar blocking their lungs' alveoli. Therefore, smokers live an unhealthy life. Moreover, they constantly inhale toxins.

We may know well what diseases smoking cause, but we never give them much attention. Let's use our imagination a little to see if we truly know about the diseases smoking causes, how well we perceive them and what information our mind ignores related to them. Relax, clear your mind. Think of a disease smoking can cause, such as lung cancer. Imagine you are in your doctor's office on a chair. He tells you with great sadness that you have lung cancer because of the excessive smoking. Fear starts overwhelming you; everything around you starts to shake. You are horrified to tell your wife or husband about this, who has asked you so many times to quit because she/he was worried. How will you explain this to your children? Will you tell them that you will no longer be there for them in the near future, that you won't be able to walk your daughter on the aisle at her wedding? How will you look them in the eyes and tell them that this happened because

because of your own weakness? They will be alone, and you will slowly be just a fading memory that in time will be forgotten. Imagine you are in a hospital bed and you have to endure various, dreadful treatments: chemotherapy, radiotherapy, etc. Imagine you can barely move from all the drugs you received. Your hair starts to fall, you are almost a skeleton; all these in front of your family's eyes that is deeply hurt and in sorrow near your bed. They don't know if they will get to have another day beside you, if they can tell you "I love you" tomorrow. You are on the bed now and you gaze into their shimmering, hopeful eyes. However, you know that the tears in their eyes show you that they know they won't be seeing you anymore, anytime soon. They are horrified that you could disappear from their lives at any moment. What will happen with them after you die? What will happen to you when you disappear, when your family buries you along with all your hopes, dreams, ambitions and goals? All lost, turned to dust, and for what? All of this because you couldn't face reality and you continued living under the illusion that this might not happen to you, that you are fine and that cigarettes bring you joy and pleasure. Wake up now, stop living a lie and submit to reality!

This imaginary exercise isn't meant to scare you, but to prove you that, although you knew to what kind of disease smoking can lead and how much suffering it involves, you have hidden all these thoughts away in a deep corner of your mind while avoiding the light of truth. Don't fall prey to ignorance!

We smoke a cigarette and feel alright. We light another one up. We still feel well, so clearly we can continue this habit. People smoke and tend to live under the impression that nothing bad will happen. The false illusion of health is being created. There is no point in thinking about diseases, since no harm has happened to us yet. There is no point to load our mind with fear and negative information. Our brain seeks to lie to us and determines us to ignore the reality surrounding smoking – which isn't very pleasant. We have smoked, everything is fine and we think that everything will go on like this forever. A few extra cigarettes won't do us any harm. But it never actually stops; a few extra cigarettes here, a few extra there and then it turns into a whole life of unhealthy smoking. You never stop. Although the body weakens with the passing of the years, it still doesn't alarm us that our health has declined. Actually, as we have progressively destroyed our health, we cannot actually imagine how a healthy person feels like. We imagine that they feel exactly like us, and we can't notice we are actually weakened and ill. In time, our mind doesn't get any brighter either. . The cigarettes have integrated themselves into our life, they are part of it now, and not having them would be like not being able to eat.

Once we do get really sick at this point, we can't but just look back with horror and realise what a stupid mistake we have made – if we still have time to do so.

Remember, you don't get sick instantly from one cigarette. It's not like Russian roulette where you shoot once, no bullet left the barrel so you made it. Everything happens progressively. The cells are deprived of nutritive substances, the body does not receive enough oxygen, and you allow the toxins to live in your body like in a hotel: some enter, some leave, some are there for a while. The consequences of a permanent unhealthy lifestyle aren't visible today or tomorrow, but in time, without you even noticing your decline. Believe me: you aren't healthy now, as good as you might feel and as much as you might try to lie to yourself. Actually, if you have paid attention to what you have read so far, you can convince yourself that you aren't. You have inhaled a lot of carcinogenic substances so far. You have already abused your body with frequent, artificially-induced cortisol, adrenaline and other hormones that are being activated by smoking.

Our mind refers to external subterfuges if it gets tired or has lack of ideas and reasons to make us continue smoking. Many people hear tales about others that have been smoking their entire life. They even made it to 80-90 and have died with "a cigarette in their mouth, from natural death".

These are just some rare cases that we tend to give importance to, but why don't you look at the other thousands of cases where smokers don't get to live this much and die in excruciating pain? Your mind ignores them and regards them as mere "statistics", numbers that we don't even give value to. It's much easier to ease our mind with the happy cases. We see only the achievements of the few, not the failures of the many. This is a way the mind works. It averts the bad to protect us. We repress our fear of disease and we don't know why. The fear of quitting smoking right now is bigger than the fear of a possible, future, incomprehensible disease. The truth is that you are already sick. You have the sickness of smoking, which crushes your life slowly like a cancer, with bad smells, useless spending and tiredness. Only this is easily treatable compared to other diseases. We will see how by going further through this book together.

WHAT HAPPENS AFTER THE LAST CIGARETTE?

It's hard for us to quit. Maybe we don't spend much on cigarettes and we can afford this expense, so we can't come up with a motivational factor for this. Sometimes we may not even believe that it will make a big difference if we quit. I mean, we do feel fine, what could be better? It's ok to think this way until now. After so many years of smoking, our body has slowly and unnoticeably degenerated. We always feel tired, but we think it's just because of our lifestyle, lack of sleep, or simply because that's how a human feels like. We can't realise that the fault lies in cigarettes, because we can't perceive a better life than what we already have. The cigarettes have reduced the quality of our lives so slowly that we began to think that it's normal to feel this way. Maybe sometimes, when you couldn't smoke for many hours and the body started to eliminate at least a few of the toxins, you had a glimpse of what life could be, you felt the wonderful "breeze" of freedom while inhaling simple air instead of tobacco smoke. Nevertheless, you continued smoking and all that glimmering hope disappeared.

So what happens after your last cigarette? Well, after 20 minutes only, the body starts rebuilding itself. It sounds incredible, but if you understood anything I have written in the previous pages, how harmful a cigarette is and if you are familiar with basic biology, you won't be that surprised anymore. Your pulse and blood pressure return to normal values. Blood flow starts to improve and your limbs start warming up (yes, cold feet and hands could be owed to cigarettes, which can cause low blood flow).

Cigarettes contain many toxins, including a toxic gas called carbon monoxide. This gas can be fatal in big doses, because it stops the oxygen from entering the lungs and blood. Therefore, the heart needs to beat faster to transport enough oxygen to the body. After 12 hours, the carbon monoxide levels in your bloodstream drop down, you won't feel too tired anymore and you breathe easier. You will feel the need to smoke at this point. You can chew sugarless gum or drink a lot of water to fight the cravings.

After 24 hours, blood pressure drops, and along with it the risk of heart disease and blood clots. The lungs start to clean themselves through constant coughing, eliminating harmful substances and residue. If you smoke a pack a day, you are twice as exposed to heart diseases than a non-smoker.

After 48 hours, your taste and smell improve. Smoking affects your nervous endings that are responsible for receiving olfactory and gustatory signals. In other words, it diminishes your ability to smell and taste. After only 48 hours, these nerve endings start to heal. The body enters a detoxification phase. The lungs continue to expel harmful residues. The bad part is that now you should be feeling the worst effects of withdrawal, if you don't listen to your body's needs. In the next chapters you will learn how to fight these feelings, even eliminate or avoid them, provided that you follow my instructions with maximum seriousness and defeat the part of your conservative mind. If you are a heavy smoker, you might feel dizzy because you are not used to a bigger amount of oxygen in your blood. Don't worry, this is normal and healthy. Your appetite increases as well.

After three days without tobacco, your body's nicotine reserves are close to zero. You will be healthier, but now the withdrawal could turn out to be unbearable. A lot of people become easily irritable in this stage and could experience headaches. The best part is that your energy levels increase a lot, so you can perform various activities that can easily distract you from your need to smoke.

The most positive changes inside your body occur in the first 3 months. After only a few weeks, you will barely have any desire to smoke and the chance of you lighting up another cigarette is highly improbable. Don't worry, it doesn't take 3 months to get rid of withdrawal, but it all depends on you. It can last only a few days, up to a week, or maybe for your entire life if you aren't determined to quit for good. Some say they haven't experienced any kind of withdrawal. Your lungs start getting stronger, your blood flows easier, you can engage in physical activity without shortness of breath. You will be surprised to see how resilient you are now; you might even feel like you have never ever smoked before.

After nine months, you will notice major improvements. Your lungs are mostly healed. After a year, the risk of a heart attack is reduced to half. This might not seem much, but think about it! Now, while you are still smoking, the risk of a heart attack is at a maximum level, so any improvement is a step forward.

After five years, the body has healed itself completely. The arteries and blood vessels have dilated and the cells have been properly fed. The risk of a heart attack is the same as for a person that has never smoked before, and the probability of you making any tobacco-related cancer is reduced to half.

Is it too late? No!

Don't get discouraged, the healing process might take long but you can see other, unmentioned improvements to your health and body in just a few days. It's very important that you take action as soon as possible. As long as you live, it's not too late to start a non-smoking life, regardless of your age. Do a great joy to your loved ones and the people that care for you. They might not even realise themselves how harmful smoking is and in what kind of danger you throw yourself with every puff. You're not only risking ruining your own life through smoking, but theirs too. Financial improvements will be also noticed. Maybe you can afford to smoke, and maybe you are healthy right now. But what if the time comes when you can't afford smoking anymore? What if you get ill? Will you be able to quit then, to resist withdrawal and fight more battles? Better quit now, while you are still able, rather than when something unexpected might strike you. You'll see; things aren't always as they seem to be because smoking can cause a chain reaction. Who knows how many wonderful things you have already missed because of smoking or how many more will come to be missed if you continue? Maybe if you had never smoked, you would have done something more interesting with the money. Maybe, if you had had all of the extra energy each day, today you wouldn't have sobbed at all the opportunities you have missed regarding the projects you never felt like starting. You surely have missed a lot because of the tiredness caused by smoking. But don't despair! You still have a lot of time to fix this, and the sudden energy wave you will experience as a new non-smoker will make you recover. Prepare yourself for a chain of changes. We live in modern times; you can easily adapt to the new lifestyle and embrace progress. The joy you will feel upon quitting smoking will be so big that you will not consider it a sacrifice anymore.

The body periodically regenerates its cells. You get hurt, you heal. You may have drowned your lungs with smoke and intoxicated your body, but from the ashes of your smoked cigarettes you will rise like a phoenix, ready to face any challenges life brings, with your newly-found determination, ambition, discipline and strength.

THE PSYCHOLOGICAL FACTOR

You have finished the previous chapter and now you know that smoking is harmful, poisonous. Maybe you knew it before, but now you can better understand why it is harmful, so you will be able to fight it easier. However, I bet you still aren't convinced of this. Although you are aware of the harmful effects smoking has upon your body, you still continue to do it. The question is: why? Our study has not ended yet. Until we get to the practical part in which you will prepare for the life of a non-smoker, you have to understand the psychological addiction a cigarette can cause, so you will be able to fight the addiction on all fronts.

Nowadays, over a billion people smoke. Tobacco and obesity are the lead causes of premature death. We commit ourselves to unhealthy habits due to our genetic inheritance, environment, friends and the mass-media. It is hard to cast away smoking when most of the information we receive regarding cigarettes and smoking is, in a way, positive. It is even harder if our own mind hides the negative aspects of smoking deep into our subconscious and occasionally, slightly remembers to scold us when we feel guilty.

Maybe there is a way to break down these invisible barriers inside our mind, a "key" with which we can open the door and let the truth come to light. The "key" is represented by all of our choices, beliefs, wills and decisions we take against these vices. These cause our inner worries; and an old proverb says: "The problem is not the problem itself, but our attitude towards it". In our case, the problem isn't actually the nicotine, but the attention we give to its consequences. Yes, nicotine might make us feel withdrawal, but it only has that great power over ourselves as long as we allow it. We can ignore the harmful effects of smoking and give in to the temptation of lighting up another cigarette or we can decide not to let ourselves get manipulated any longer, especially by ourselves. We will fight this vice off with the information we get.

Our decisions. They will allow us to win over our temptation to smoke. Maybe we won't even feel any temptation if we convince ourselves well enough that we don't want to continue smoking. We aren't talking here about willpower, but about treating temptation as it is: a simple disposable desire and removing it in the simplest manner. We open ourselves up to it; acknowledge its existence. We observe and analyse it. The more we fight temptation, the more we think about it. The more we think about it, the more intense it will get and we risk giving in. We have to accept that it will dissipate in time and it will open up doors to new possibilities, new pathways in life. It will make us tougher.

WHY DO WE CONTINUE SMOKING?

Most of us work automatically. We wake up, we smoke. We make coffee, we smoke. We take a break from work, we smoke. Cigarettes are part of our daily routine; we light them up out from automatism without even noticing the gesture. It seems natural for us to smoke while we drink coffee, while we drive, while we talk on the phone or drink alcohol. We can't imagine a lunchbreak without a cigarette; we can't even seem to think without smoking. We realize how much we smoke, but we don't give it too much thought. The subconscious does its duty: every time, it signals an occurring event that is similar to a previous one when we have smoked. This is called a trigger. If we don't smoke this time, we end up feeling like there is something missing, we aren't doing things right, we aren't as efficient as before. But from now on, before lighting up a cigarette, proceed otherwise: ask yourself if you truly need it or this is an automated gesture. After all the damage tobacco has done so far, do you really want to continue smoking?

People live under the impression that smoking relaxes them. Many people smoke because they work a lot and they need a small break, to clear up their mind. They seek to relax to disconnect from the world for a short period of time. The truth is that the dopamine release from smoking gives us a pleasant sensation throughout the body and may calm us down. As you already know, dopamine is released every time you diminish your cravings with a cigarette. The mind, through the subconscious, thanks you for handling the issue efficiently. What the subconscious doesn't know is that cigarettes you had before this one have actually caused the cravings you have experienced. It is your duty, the conscious you, to teach the subconscious this through various techniques you will learn throughout this book. One such technique is to break the link between coffee and cigarettes, or by not smoking while talking on the phone; break the habits and resist these triggers. The simple abstinence from smoking until your subconscious learns that you don't really need cigarettes can do well too.

We let ourselves influenced by circumstance. Anywhere we look, we see smokers. We see tough guys smoking on TV. Some smoke after making love, others in sign of victory after a hard battle. We like their personality and we have the impression that we can be just like them. The only thing that separates their coolness from ours seems to be a cigarette. So we end up copying the smoking gesture. We are brainwashed, at its own permission because our brain cannot easily filter what we see, and cannot always distinguish good from evil, especially in the case of smoking. We are rarely provided by the mass-media with negative information related to smoking, and then, our brain ignores it completely. Maybe it does so to protect us from the negative emotions we might experience. It's also possible that we simply to do not offer them enough care, we already feel guilty for smoking, we don't need an external source to further scold us.

Another cause for smoking is boredom. However, the idea itself that smoking drives away monotony is an illusion. This means that all non-smokers lead boring lives. The "activity" of smoking does nothing but to fill the empty moments in our lives, and instead of finding a productive activity, we tend to procrastinate, or in this case, to harm our lungs. Smoking may fill up these voids in our daily routine, but you accomplish nothing by doing so. On the contrary, you actually waste time that could have been spent more effectively, creatively or simply with your loved ones that might need your presence more than you might realise. Have you forgotten about your live goals? What about your ambitions and dreams? If you really need a break, you can engage in procrastinating, but in a constructive way: watch funny videos to lighten up your spirit and mood, or simply lie down and meditate; something constructive surely will come from your thoughts.

We tend to live under the impression that cigarettes offer us some "alone time", so we can simply escape from the world, meditate in peace and quiet and reflect upon our problems. Now, as I am a non-smoker, I cannot seem to realise how I was tend to think this way. Smoking consumes, among other things, time. How can I have more time when, actually, I am wasting it by smoking?

The "alone time" exists anyway, but we use smoking as an excuse to walk away, to take a break, or to hide in a quiet corner all by ourselves, while adding toxins into our body.

Smokers consider that they need will to quit. It's true. The main way to quit is the desire to take action, and so did you by reading this book. You cannot actually quit without wanting to do it. I mean you might, but you would go through horrible withdrawal, both physically and mentally. Even if you biologically "unlearn" to smoke, you will psychologically be haunted for the rest of your life by thinking that you gave up a big pleasure in life. Your mind has been manipulated by nicotine for far too long to think otherwise, and when you deprive your body of nicotine, abruptly and without preparations, it will turn against you with a heavy withdrawal, like a baby crying out loud.

Some live under the impression that smoking is a source of energy. The truth is that the phenomena that happen in our body while smoking is so slow that in fact it actually builds up fatigue without us noticing. We get used to feeling tired; we consider it normal as a result of our busy lives. We may also think that every person feels this way; it's simply the way life is. When we smoke, as you have already learnt, our body experiences a shock and receives adrenaline and a false feeling of dynamism. I can assure you that you don't get as much energy as you would by keeping your lungs and blood clean from tobaccos toxins.

Many so-called help methods available in other books and sources of information list the reasons why you shouldn't smoke: health, money, unpleasant smell etc. These are rather ineffective methods to help others quit. All smokers are aware of these, and many other reasons, but they still continue to smoke. Why? Because smoking relaxes you, it helps you focus on your task, eases the stress, helps you get rid of boredom and, above all, it is simply "pleasant" – these are serious reasons not to quit, I admit. But let's suppose these reasons mentioned above aren't real. Let's suppose smoking doesn't really bring these benefits, but rather it creates us a foggy mind, hindering our focus, it provides anxiety rather than alleviating stress and makes you procrastinate and push your tasks aside. Would you still smoke? Of course not. What you don't realise is – probably because you're smoking and nicotine is pulling strings in your mind like a puppeteer – is that a cigarette doesn't really offer anything, but the lack of nicotine makes you long for what's missing. In fact, tobacco doesn't really provide any of the previously listed benefits, but suppresses all those feelings, and leaves us with scrapes that in time we come to consider as good results from cigarettes. It's a vicious cycle you are in, from which you can escape very hard unless you really want to quit.

It's important for you to understand why you aren't currently very enthusiastic to quit smoking and why you smoke in the first place; I mean your own reasons if you cannot relate to the earlier mentioned reasons. Analyse your own reasons, break them down and try to find why you are deceiving yourself by smoking. If the reason is simply because you like it, well, think again and try harder. You may like it, but life is more pleasant without it, trust me, trust the other non-smokers you see enjoying their lives.

The first step to free yourself from such a harmful habit –you might also call it addiction, obsession – is to understand that what you consider pleasure is just a temporary reduction of an emotional discomfort, an illusion induced by the very act of smoking. When you'll manage to free yourself and when you'll realise that you were caught up in nicotine's trap, when your subconscious wants to cure you from this habit, then the impulse of resuming will disappear and, along with it, the conviction that you actually like to smoke. When this will happen, there will be no more risk of relapsing. The key to having free will is to remove the things you wrongly feel you have to do, in this case: smoking. Don't live a life dominated by compulsive behaviour and negative stimuli.

WHO DO YOU GIVE UP SMOKING FOR?

Firstly, remove any thought from your mind that you are quitting for somebody else and that you will do this "sacrifice" for a loved one or for your family. You are quitting for nobody else but yourself, because you will feel better, you will save money, you will get in shape easier and you will generally live a healthier life. Eventually you can say you quit for the sake of someone beloved, but in the end you still do it for yourself. You have to look at quitting this way; otherwise, it won't help you. Our mind tends to do exactly the opposite, when it comes to do "sacrifices", especially for other people. It likes routine, it's the way the mind has been programmed, and any forced exit from this routine will activate its conservatory strength. Therefore, don't force yourself into quitting; rather help your mind embrace this idea so it will want to create a new healthy-living routine.

At a certain time, our will to smoke will dominate any feeling for our loved ones, but the love for the self and personal growth should be stronger, especially due to our survival instincts. When your mind will learn and really understand what happens to your body and life because of smoking, it will surely assist you in your attempt to quit. You know it very well that there are times when you challenge and argue with your spouse only to retreat and smoke, especially if you are denied to smoke, or frowned upon. This is why it is best to quit only for your own sake. If you do it for other people, you might end up smoking in secret, to hide the shame or relapse. In the end, you will get caught. You will avoid people and thus also live with the stress that you will get caught, which amplifies the need to smoke. You will develop resentment towards those that stop you to smoke.

FEAR

Fear is the main reason most smokers don't quit for good, even if they do know and understand the negative biological and psychological effects smoking has upon their body. Fear represses our ambition and hinders any attempt to quit smoking. We are afraid it will be hard (it won't) that the discomfort accompanied by withdrawal will be a torture (it won't), that the effort isn't worth it (it is) and that we are not ready to endure it (you have the ability to do anything you propose to yourself). Maybe you don't have time to focus on your life while dealing with withdrawal. Only thinking about withdrawal it somehow makes you want to light a cigarette up. Maybe the fear of considering or imagining a life without cigarettes is overwhelming. What will you do in your breaks? What will you do while your friends will smoke around you? It seems like a long, chaotic time is yet to come. You are wrong. You will proceed as all ex-smokers did so well: adapt to the new lifestyle. It's like changing jobs, maybe confusing at first, but after a while you get the hang of it and carry your tasks on without any thought. Don't let yourself guided by negative thoughts!

After a period of time without smoking, you will enjoy breathing without tar burdening your lungs, but also the more vitality you'll get. You won't have any more problems in the future. Maybe you tried quitting in the past, and you didn't succeed. The feelings and moods you went through amplified your fear. Now you are "traumatized" of everything you might endure. It seems like there isn't any solution to your case. You have tried and know how hard it is; impossible you might think. You feel like you are predestined to smoke for your entire life.

Failure occurs only when you stop trying. If you had resisted the urge to smoke for a few extra seconds maybe, today you would have been a non-smoker. I can honestly tell you that you probably gave in a few moments before any craving would disappear for good.

Now that you have acquired all this knowledge through this book you won't fail anymore. Your neuronal connections related to quitting and the negative effects of cigarettes have been strengthened; you know how smoking works now, how it slowly traps and torments you. Have a little more patience! Maybe you start realising that, one day, you really have to quit. Don't let yourself be filled by fear. It will block your perception over reality. You will continue smoking as long as you look at the quitting process with fear. Instead, focus on the positive aspects from quitting and embrace them. Try viewing the process as a positive change in your life. Because that's what it actually is. Wonderful things are waiting for you just around the corner, you simply have to change the direction you are going and take the turn, rather than going the same way you always went and that never got you anywhere.

The fear of losing our focus when quitting is another reason we easily don't quit. Our lives are so busy, we try to finish our projects on time and we surely don't need additional disturbances to affect our lives, like withdrawal. Our jobs depend on our focus, our lives and our family. As you have learned so far, the impression that cigarettes offer us a better focus is just an illusion. We try not to get distracted by anything so we can finish our projects. The more intense we work, the more we feel the need to light up another cigarette to help us stay focused. You may now notice that this time too, as before, the previous cigarette actually created your inability to focus. This is paradoxical. You don't want to quit so you can maintain your focus, but nicotine addiction makes you long for smoking and stops you from fulfilling your tasks. Sometimes you might also feel no need to smoke, but you can't actually get anything done, not even thinking, without having a cigarette. After all this time, your mind has been programmed to do any action whilst smoking. If you think about it, you are experiencing a dilemma. You leave your work aside to go smoking and clearing up your mind. You calm down and new ideas come to mind. If you notice, you aren't doing anything else but allocating some of your time to meditate, analyse your situation, but unfortunately also while intoxicating yourself.

You don't need a cigarette to be able to think clearly. You simply need "alone time", in which you can meditate and reflect upon your tasks. This kind of time seems to be granted by cigarettes when taking a break to smoke, but you can take time off anyways. However, your mind is currently associating this "free" time with cigarettes and lives under the impression that you cannot handle the situation without a smoke. And if you do it, you will think about smoking, which doesn't support your idea of quitting. When you quit and try to take a break, to think, ponder, meditate, your mind will bother you with thoughts like: "You used to smoke at this point; maybe you should smoke now, too. You used to have good ideas while smoking; so have a cigarette, maybe some might come now". While these thoughts are bothering you, you'll notice that you are unable to actually reflect or meditate, to think about your projects and tasks, so you come to admit that you do need a cigarette to focus. But yet again, the lack of focus is still created by the previous cigarette. So, for the sake of finishing your work, you give in and light one up. After a while, you will need more nicotine, your dopamine receptors get worn out, so a single cigarette won't allow you to calm down and focus as you did before. You are blocking you arteries with nicotine and other toxic substances that deprive your brain of oxygen in the meantime. This clearly does not help you think, although your increased blood pressure makes you think otherwise.

The fact that you are always horrified whenever the idea of quitting comes up doesn't have a biological cause; rather a psychological one, based on previous, failed quitting attempts. This is why you hear that some managed to quit in one shot, easily. They might have had luck, or went through a hard withdrawal without admitting it, but they finally succeeded. If they hadn't done it, their future attempts to quit would have been compromised. Do not worry though; in your past attempts you didn't own this helpful book, and you didn't have my words as a friend and guide to help you quit. Trust me: you can do it, and you will. Just remember that if you do experience any fear in trying again, your past failed attempts and experiences with withdrawal have been printed into your subconscious, which is currently trying to hinder you from quitting so you won't have to face those challenges again. Just convince your subconscious, through reading this book, and through meditation, that those are things belonging the past, and that this time, you are armed and ready. In a future chapter, we will talk about the subconscious, about its wide power and how to harness it to quit smoking effectively and with ease. You will then understand the way it works, the patterns it has created, which triggers access to those patterns that make you want to smoke. While discovering them, you will turn them against smoking.

THE PSYCHOLOGICAL IMPACT

Smoking isn't only unhealthy and harmful for your body, but it also affects our psyche. You get addicted to nicotine and react every time your body asks for it. The subconscious will assimilate your enslaved reaction to tobacco and will make you believe that you are powerless and lacking willpower. This is a direct negative aspect of smoking, upon your mind. An indirect one is that smoking creates fatigue, it fills your body up with toxins and, at the end, it hinders you from doing any physical exercise. Thus, you are never in shape, you might even have a few extra pounds and visceral fat, which makes you unhappy about the way you look. You start constantly nagging about yourself and the unpleasant look you have in your own eyes. You never really feel like you appreciate how you look and end up living a life that, in the bottom of your soul, you detest. Instead of doing something about that, you smoke, out of habit and anxiety of your looks maybe, which further hinders you to take any action upon it. You start working after you put the cigarette out. But you never do light just one; sometimes it's two or more, until you end up watching funny animal videos on social networks. Maybe you never brought the problem of how much smoking really affects you up, but, if you start thinking about it and look at things from the outside, you will notice that you waste a lot of time smoking – even more than you can imagine, actually. Synthesising, you will understand that, in fact, you are making a fool out of yourself through smoking. You complain about everything whilst engaging in smoking. One way or another, almost every negative aspect in your life can be traced back to smoking.

Our mouths smell unpleasantly, our teeth turn yellow. We throw ash everywhere around us, create a mess, and we spend most of our time next to filthy ashtrays. People stigmatize us, so we can't smoke in lots of public places. Mostly near garbage bins. We are indeed marginalized as smokers. We get enslaved by a vice that does nothing but to slowly squeeze our life out. It makes us tired. We want to stop smoking, but we can't and we start feeling guilty. Do you notice the weight you are putting on yourself, all the negative feelings, emotions and all the mood swings you are going through, due to smoking? What burden do we put upon our souls? What impact do you think all these have upon your psyche, your life? They make you seem weak, unable to resist temptations. You aren't capable to abstain from something that you and everybody else around you know slowly kills you. Are you able to actually do anything with your life, if you can't even save it from certain, unavoidable death? You feel pity – and disgust–for yourself. Generally, smokers despise themselves, knowing how much harm cigarettes do, and indirectly they end up despising themselves because of the inactivity smoking promotes. Do you think that, by having such an impression about yourself, you will be able to face bigger and more complex struggles? No. You become your own psychological captive.

Don't feel this way anymore. What has been is over, but what will come will be greater. The fact that you are reading this book is a good sign. Your ambition will rise like a snowball rolling down a mountain. In the end, it gets so big and strong that it will remove anything in its path. Now, all you need is the certainty that you will succeed quitting.

It's not sure that we will get ill or we will die from smoking (another fear that is weighing down on our souls). We don't have the certainty we will succeed in quitting. But, what we do have is the certainty that smoking relaxes us. All smokers smoke so they can amplify an emotional, positive, state or to attenuate a negative one. You can have the certainty that it calms you down, but also it is offering you the unpleasant sensation of withdrawal. Change the way you view smoking and accept the facts as they are. Even if you don't see a disease on the horizon, it's there and you can be sure its spectre won't disappear as long as you don't stop feeding this vice. With will and discipline, you can accomplish anything.

THE SUBCONSCIOUS

The mind has two parts:
1. The subconscious: the automate function and the information storage function;
2. The conscious: the function that takes decisions and adds them to the subconscious. The adding of new information to the subconscious is done instantly if the information provided is new, or slowly and progressive, through constant repetition, if it enters into a conflict with information already existing in your subconscious. If you repeat information, you integrate it faster to the subconscious, when at a certain part, it turns

into automatism. Hence the saying: Practice makes perfect.

Every person knows, at least to a lesser extent, what the subconscious is and how it can solve the problems we are addressing and that come upon us. It's possible to write many books regarding this topic, how the subconscious works, how important it is for us, but also how dangerous it becomes if we leave it unattended, prey to the information we collect during our waking days and without filtering them. The conscious mind exists due to this reason. They both work together and it helps the subconscious process information, while the subconscious presents the stored information to the conscious, so it can be able to compare the new information and either assimilate it, or dispose of it.

The subconscious determines our reactions to external factors, but also to internal ones as well – that we can't see or feel. It determines the pulse and sensations such as anger. It feeds the cells, decomposes and digests food. The whole "automative" process of our bodies, brains and minds occurs through the subconscious. It also "automatizes" the act of smoking, and you will soon see how.

I will not describe much of the conscious mind's functions, because you already know that you shouldn't be smoking. But why aren't you quitting then? Because, in the meantime, with each cigarette you have smoked, you have integrated into your subconscious the act of smoking and the false benefits that you think it brings. The conscious is some sort of a filter for the subconscious, but once the information that smoking is good, pleasant and soothing lingers in the subconscious and is stronger than the information about it being harmful, it will still let both "bubbles" of information feed. But from now on you will have to focus on feeding the other bubble.

The subconscious fulfills a role that the conscious mind cannot manipulate; one that has been embedded into our DNA: it takes care of the body. For instance, it maintains temperature at the same level and makes the heart pump blood in a certain rhythm, making our pulse rise when needed. Your body is like a machine that is being controlled by the subconscious. However strong the subconscious might appear, it cannot create anything new, neither have a free will, rather it respects a simple "procedure" list that it has stored, and constantly modifies and adapts to new information acquired. We won't talk about the general role of the subconscious, but upon its function of creating and identifying patterns that we use in our daily routine.

The subconscious is like a memory bank. Practically, it has unlimited capacity and stores everything that happens to you. The subconscious role is to store and to retrieve information. Through it you react to external stimuli the way you were programmed to; everything you do, meets an already existing pattern inside you, a pattern that has been built over the years. This is why it is so important to repeat positive affirmations as lots of people say. It is because you are reprogramming your thought process through adding positive data. Activities like reading motivational quotes for instance, quotes that inspire you, have a huge impact on people and determine them to think positive on the long run. Whenever you focus on inspiring ideas, your subconscious will begin to implement them by either creating a new pattern, or improving the old one. While adding such new, positive information to your subconscious, you pave new roads, or rebuild older ones making them more visible, and the subconscious begins to remove the negative information in time, making room for new, empowering information.

The subconscious is subjective. It doesn't think and reason on its own, but it listens to the commands received by the conscious mind. Imagine that the subconscious is the garden and the conscious the gardener. If the latter plants seeds, they will grow into trees with deep roots that in time will bear fruits meant to feed the living. Thus, you can see how important the seeds (the positive thoughts) are in your mind (garden).

All habits, your way of thinking and acting are stored in the subconscious. It memorizes the comfort zones and works to keep you inside them. I mean, who can blame it? If you survive in such comfort zones, why would it bother to remove you out of them and put you in danger? That is why, it is important to always establish a purpose, a goal, and to fulfil it with discipline, whether you like it or not.

Be productive and focus on your goals until they are included to your comfort zone that your subconscious so preciously protects. The key here is to use your conscious mind. You can rationally acknowledge change or hard work should be done, but the subconscious' role is to simply keep you alive, so any additional effort is seen as useless, until proven otherwise for the subconscious.

The subconscious creates emotional and physical discomfort every time you want and try to do something new, namely every time you try and change its patterns. Such discomfort is a sign that you have activated your subconscious.

Its tendency is to not let you easily walk out of these patterns, and this is the reason why you tend to give up bad habits so hard. However, when you learn to form patterns with the help of your conscious mind, you cultivate the power of habit and you intentionally create new comfort zones to which the subconscious will adapt. These new subconscious areas can also be straining. It doesn't really matter; once they form a pattern, your subconscious will no longer see them as such; rather it will see them as new "comfort areas". For instance, when you start physical exercise at first, you must do it consciously, and the physiological pain could wear you down. But as you do it repeatedly, it becomes part of you, of your life, of your subconscious, and so it will adapt until you will do exercise not as a compulsoriness but as a habit. This can be done until the point where you no longer do physical exercise; your subconscious will beg you to do it, to keep you into that newly established, habitual comfort area.

It's possible that the subconscious might try to pull you back once you try something new, something different than what it is used to. The mere thought of doing new things gives you a feeling of unease and unrest. To be able to evolve outside of this comfort area, you need will and the ability to accept the fact that you might feel weird and uncomfortable doing things for the first time. Once you accept these things through your conscious, it will be easier for you to proceed, because you know it doesn't harm you; at least that's what you are trying to signal to your subconscious. The possible retention you might feel is just a natural response from your subconscious to the idea of novelty.

Your automated mechanisms and gestures are guided by one of the most powerful inner forces: the subconscious. Remember how you learned to ride your bicycle? How at first you paid attention to every move you made, each stroke of the pedal? Surely you were tense; you consciously measured each move you had to make. It was very difficult to synchronize each move, to hold your balance and even to go a small distance without falling. When you did fall, you might have been tempted to quit or you were at least afraid of trying to get on it again.

You were afraid that you might fall again and were tempted to give up, but maybe someone encouraged you to push your limits and, in the end, you succeeded. In time, you thought about the process and actions you did while riding the bike less and less, while your movements became more natural. Now you are able to paddle by instinct.

This also happens when you try to quit. The subconscious plays and important role in eliminating – or keeping – your fear. It can consider sudden changes in your body as a threat, like smoking for instance, especially when it notices that they cause you anxiety, and will try to urge you to continue smoking. But, once you consciously resist this urge, and the temptation to smoke, just like you faced your fear of falling off the bicycle, you will adapt to it. The transition from the conscious mind to the subconscious is slow and takes time, practice and full understanding of the phenomena. Don't worry, you won't "fall"; I'm here to support you.

Once we understand how the triggers in our brain work, we can convince the subconscious to do what we desire, to change as we like and do what we consciously know is best for us. This is possible only through knowledge, through the accumulation of information. In the case of a smoker, the necessary information is held in this book. You are currently using your conscious mind to read and extract the meanings of these words, while the subconscious is preoccupied with working "behind the scenes", absorbing or repelling information based on the way in which you perceive your surroundings and the data you have collected throughout your life. This perception exists since you were a child. The subconscious absorbed each experience in your life like a sponge. When you were young, and didn't have much life experience; the subconscious didn't really reject much information as it had nothing to compare it to. It simply accepted most data as truths. This also happens now when you receive novelty information that doesn't conflict with what you already know; you simply accept the information as such. That is why, we are, for instance, predisposed to "fake news" and do not check the information unless we have the slightest doubt about a conflictual information.

This attitude can create problems. Because you are told many times that you cannot succeed in doing something, the subconscious keeps this negative information and will use it every time you are willing to act, slowing you down and demotivating you. As an adult, you think you can eliminate such negative information that is presented to you, but it really isn't that easy. Even if your subconscious is mostly filled with ambition, a repetition of negative information can outgrow the positive ones in your brain and, in time, slowly determine you to fail. Everything is being stocked inside the subconscious. Did you ever try to accomplish something in life, only to fail mostly because of yourself? In other words, did you ever try and fail only because you gave up? It is important you understand that you are not likely to fail. Most likely, you only have a few old messages in your subconscious that come in conflict with the new conditions you are trying to create. This means, if you consciously affirm for a few times that you can accomplish something, your mind-set will begin to shift, and if you do it long enough, it will change for good or tilt on the positive side. It's like having a bag with, let's say, 10 black spheres that represent all the negative information you have over your abilities, and 10 white ones that represent all the positive information you have over your abilities. The chance of extracting either colour is 50%. But if you add positive affirmations, white spheres, to the bag, the probability of extracting such a colour rises. It rises with each sphere, until the probability of extracting a negative thought is close to zero. This is just an allegory so you can imagine my idea. The brain is much more complex than this, but for the sake of moving forward, use this perception.

The fact that once you understand this and focus on improving your perception and view of life is wonderful. This means you can accomplish anything if you allow enough time to work on your subconscious. If, in the past, you sabotaged yourself with negative information regarding quitting smoking, now that you understand this mechanism, your chances of sabotaging yourself decrease, and by the end of this book you will be surely able to reprogram your mind-set regarding this subject completely. But this won't work simply with my help; you are the key factor in this process. You have to really want this change, not simply read about it here. Tell yourself that you will succeed.

Once we understand that our actions reconfigure our neuronal connections, it will be easier to take measures against our bad habits. Hereby though, we risk falling into a trap: we know how to change, and we know we can change, so we tend to keep our habits for a while longer because we think we can do it any time soon. The information you are receiving while reading is fresh now, so you have to act upon smoking and start the quitting process during this time. If you allow more days to pass after finishing reading this book, you will surely be struck by external information, or even self-created information, about how you should continue smoking. The brain will start strengthening your habit to smoke, while slowly forgetting about this newly-found ambition to quit. The most intelligent people are able to fall into this trap; watch out! You aren't better than any other people just because you have the knowledge and potential to change. You also have to take action. Act upon all things progressively. Potential is just potential until action is taken.

The subconscious can solve any problem if it's properly programmed. Otherwise, it can create other problems and cause reactions that we might not like. The subconscious has shaped our way of reaction, and only in it lays the capacity to change it. Don't feed it with negative data, because it might consider it positive. Remember: it cannot make the difference between good and bad. Don't think that you can quit, but think that you will.

Before finding out how to program your subconscious further, and make it support our conscious ambition to quit smoking, you have to understand that this reprogramming is a continuous process that has to be dealt with daily, with each activity carried out and with each stimulus received. But be careful: if a new experience comes into conflict with information that is already stored in your subconscious, it will either reject it, or it will rephrase it in such a way that it coincides with the present information. This means that it will make you hear what you want to hear, what it wants to hear what it already knows. This is why change can be hard, but simply don't drift away from your goal.

Let's consider that you find yourself physically unattractive and a person appears that seems to show interest in you. Your first reaction would be to think that the person either taunts you, or is making a joke. Instead of accepting the fact that the person likes you, you reject it and sabotage the possibility of a relationship. This is how it works with smoking, too. If you are tempted to look for reasons to continue smoking, although you know it doesn't do you well, if you reject the ideas presented to you by this book and consider that smoking doesn't really affect your life and health, think again.

We will focus only on a few methods through which you can reprogram your subconscious. Countless books have been written covering this subject, but we will focus mainly on those that fit our goal: helping you quit. It's better to grant more care to these methods, rather than diluting the effort through hundreds of inefficient ways or fighting concomitantly with other negative factors in your subconscious. The main technique assumes respecting and acknowledging all the information in this book and correlating them with what you need to do to quit.

IMPROVING THE SUBCONSCIOUS

Offer the subconscious a new pattern on which it can act. In this chapter, I will give you a few pieces of advice on how to change your subconscious way of processing data related to smoking, like in any aspect of your life. Don't forget! We are currently focusing only on smoking. Subsequently, when you become a non-smoker and if you consider that this chapter has helped you, you can read it again to help other possible problems that you might be facing.

1. The first step to make a radical change isn't necessarily thinking if it is possible to accomplish it, because you would contradict your subconscious, but if you have the will to try. You can't instantly turn from scepticism to optimism. First, you have to find out if you are capable of change or at least have the willingness to try.

2. In the quitting period, limit the negative messages you receive. If people tell you that you will not succeed, ignore them and don't interact with them until you manage to quit for good. You don't need external factors that will cut off your momentum and ruin your disposition. Surround yourself with a positive atmosphere and motivational quotes and people.

3. Make room for success in your life. Instead of declaring that you will be happy only when, for instance, you have lost 20 pounds, when you have more money or after unfortunate moments pass, repeat to yourself: "I want a better life". Allow yourself to be happy and successful without yourself feeling guilty for everything around you. After that, focus on progress and improvement.

4. Try visualising your future without a cigarette. Continue this way constantly and you will be able to rewrite the patterns that guide your life and you will get used to living without cigarettes easier. Imagine you drink coffee and drive your car, both without smoking. Imagine moments

you used to smoke, but this time without cigarettes. Thus you are creating an image of your own life without tobacco, so when you do quit, the feeling of not having cigarettes by your side won't be unfamiliar. Also, try adding emotions to these visualisations. While you imagine driving or drinking coffee without smoking, try feeling blissful, fulfilled, happy. The subconscious will absorb these information and feelings as if they were real, and will slowly shift its point of view to notice happiness, bliss and peace in such moments. Bomb your subconscious whenever you have the possibility to do so to strengthen these ties and neuronal connections. By now, I think you already have a clear image about the way the subconscious works and you know on your own how to precede further. Because it absorbs data like a sponge, you can choose what information you will allow it to see and hear, at least to what kind of information you allow yourself to be exposed to.

5. Repeat, repeat, repeat. Statements and visualization exercises don't work if you try them out only once or twice. Remember that sphere allegory I used earlier? Each time you repeat a positive affirmation, you add a white sphere to your bag of information. So to add more spheres, thus decreasing the possibility of extracting black spheres, you need to keep repeating information. Be careful! During your

day, external factors might add black spheres to your bag, even without you noticing, so remember to keep filling the bag consciously to leave no room for surprises.

Beware; you might be able to fill that "bag" with negative information by your own. Don't repeat negative statements. When you find yourself doing so, simply ward them off with positive phrases, related to the same subject. For example, if you think you have lots on your head and have no time to solve them, tell yourself: "Well, I don't have that much actually on my head. There were times when I was much busier and I did manage to finish my tasks. I will do so now, too." Unfortunately, we cannot see what lies in our subconscious. Try to develop an active self-conscious that notices when you engage in self-sabotaging behaviour and use this to add through it information in your subconscious that will change your way of thinking and improve your patterns of reaction. It is important to allow time to this reprogramming process, so you can receive the expected results. Don't expect immediate change; some of your thinking systems and patterns are already very complex and deeply rooted into your personality. Only time, repetition, patience and exercise will create change.

6. If you accept a certain suggestion while being in a state of profound relaxation, it will penetrate easier into your subconscious and become a

reality. While you are in such a state, the conscious doesn't really work, so its filters and processing work slowly and allow more information to enter the subconscious, whether good or bad. This can also happen while you are tired.

7. Imagine you have no problems, you are not struggling to quit, you don't long and will not long for anything, ever, and that is how your mind will perceive reality. Cravings are often self-induced, leaving the biological part aside, through the simple fact that we allow them to rise and to influence us further.

8. Talk about your success as a current reality, rather than a future plan. You are happy now; you are determined to quit smoking now. The moment when you have everything you need is now.

9. Let vision evolve. Don't burden your mind with the difficulties you go through, but rather reflect on your success in life, all the good things you did and are capable of doing. To be able to imagine what you want to accomplish in life is essential, because, if you don't know exactly where your goal is, you don't know how to get there.

10. Don't fill the void in your life with cigarettes, but with encouraging elements. On your way to work listen to motivational speakers instead of the news which are likely to demotivate you and make you fall into depression. Proceed likewise

when you clean up, do the dishes, cook or engage in any activity that doesn't require lots of attention.

11. Meditate as often as possible and be satisfied with what you have.

12. Remember that you shape yourself according to your company. Be careful of people surrounding you, and if you notice that they are negatively influencing you, ask yourself if it is necessary to spend the time with them, or if you should move on.

13. Identify the blockades. If your subconscious tries to block us from following something we like or desire, it means we have conflictual ideas. I admit that, while working on this book, I had some doubts. I had a lot of ambition in writing it, but from time to time the thought that maybe I am trying in vain, and nobody would read it, kept interrupting my writing. I hoped I was not wasting my time, so I stopped often and wasted time thinking if I should continue or not. I sometimes left anxiety to swallow me and I allowed negative thoughts to slow me down. Anyways, in my case, I allowed the fear of failure to stun me and make me lay on my bed helpless. When I did notice what I was doing, I would get up and continue writing. In the end, as you can see, I did continue and finished it. I told myself that I already started the project, and I will give my everything to finish it.

14. Instead of making a three, four or ten long life-

plan, make a general plan on what you wish to accomplish in life. When you create such long plans, and realise in time that you are drifting away from them or that you might not actually succeed, you could slide in a slope and end up with no progress. Plan your life in such a way that you don't really have a specific target in mind, like earning 1 million dollars in 3 years, but allowing yourself to build up any character and physical traits that you might end up earning it eventually, or that you are ready for any opportunity that might arise. Take regard for each aspect in your life that should be improved. You want to be more charismatic, to smile more often, to be happy, to engage in more physical activity and so on. Ask yourself what the ideal life would be, but take care to imagine things that are real possibilities. Don't over dream or you might end up in that slope again if you seem to get further away from your dreams in time. You would be tempted to think that having more money would simply solve your issues, but you are already struggling to be richer. Focusing on making more money, without focusing on building yourself up first so your lifestyle may allow easier access to it, won't help. You can think about how to make more money, but focus on the indirect means that make you actually happy, for instance, in being a better person, a more talkative one. This might end in opening possibilities and opportunities for you to acquire that extra income you so long for. Imagine what the best version of yourself could be and take the measures required for you to be that person. What would you spend all that money on, what would you do if you were rich? Would you do more volunteer work? You can do that too, without more money, simply helping people in ways you are able to. Would you read more? You can do it now, too. By widening your horizon, maybe new business ideas come to mind. Would you travel more? Travel in regions next to you, with less money. You surely don't need much money to do it and you can surely discover beautiful things in your area. Enjoy the little things more; they are cheap and can offer you the same amount of happiness as more money would. Don't think about how much happiness weighs in terms of money, and don't allow money to dictate the amount of pleasure you feel in your life; rather do what you can do now to make yourself happy, with what you have around you. A happier and self-loving person is more prone to greatness in time than a frustrated one of his/her own life.

As soon as nicotine enters your body and you become addicted to it, the reaction in your brain from the lack of nicotine creates withdrawal. The brain, through anxiety and stress, makes you understand that you need to smoke to cast away these feelings. Once you smoke, you feel better, you are less stressed, if at all, and you come to think that the cigarette helped. But now that you know the truth behind this and that the previous cigarette actually brought this state upon you, why are you still lighting another one up whilst knowing that the same phenomena will occur the next time? It is because you do understand that you don't need to smoke, but only on a conscious level, while your subconscious is still struggling to support the already built-in information on the joy of smoking. It doesn't help you, but you are obliged to face your daily life's problems – and you do have enough problems – you don't need the extra anxiety and stress from quitting. So you allow nicotine to keep you on its own instead of fighting against it. The subconscious has slowly learned that cigarettes generate pleasure and, if you don't take measures now to readjust your mind-set, it will keep on believing so. It will never be an optimal time to quit. If you don't manage to block this cycle, you will stay addicted for the rest of your life. Things are going slowly; we don't notice what happens. Because of this, we create the illusion that we aren't really addicted, but only that we like to smoke. We feel like it's not the stress making us smoke, but simply our will and desire to do so. You might not even notice the stress that the brain cause and that creates the need to smoke. So, if by now you really think you aren't actually addicted and you simply like to smoke, I challenge you to think again and try not to smoke for several days. If all you can think about is smoking, well then, my friend, you do have a problem and it is time to admit it. Once you admit it, all you need next is motivation, willpower and discipline.

MOTIVATION, WILLPOWER AND DISCIPLINE

These three character traits may seem alike, but there are huge differences between them. And these differences are worthy to be studied, because if one depletes and you lose your thrive, you may use the others. The most powerful one is motivation, but all of these traits are equally important in life. One cannot exist without the other; they simply don't make sense alone, like blood doesn't make any sense without the heart, and vice versa. It is important for us to study them now. Beside the fact that you can use them any time, they will help you quit smoking and remain a non-smoker for the rest of your life.

Motivation is an internal process. Whether we define it as a drive or a need, motivation is a condition inside us that desires a change, either in the self or the environment. When we tap into this well of energy, motivation endows the person with the drive and direction needed to engage with the environment in an adaptive, open-ended, and problem-solving sort of way (Reeve, 2018). Motivation for doing something is born instantly, especially when you know that at the end, or shortly after completion of the task, there is a benefit. It comes in waves and that is why it is hard to make use of it daily. You feel overwhelmed by your plans and you cannot totally respect the process of fulfilling them. There are days when you wake up full of energy, there are other days when you can barely make it out of bed. You need to learn how to maintain motivation at an optimal level, especially because you have decided to quit smoking for good. Use dopamine as often as you can. Start off with small tasks that offer you a small sense of victory and satisfaction with each completion, so that during your day you feel motivated to engage in more activities, maintaining your motivation with each successful fulfilment. A small advice: always remember what you are working hard for. Have your purpose, your goal in mind while dealing with withdrawal. Our mind tends to block everything that doesn't agree with us; for instance, instead of working, lying on the bed seems as a better alternative. This is how delay and procrastination are born.

Imagine a red shirt. You will probably think about it for a few seconds, until something else distracts your attention and you forget about it. But what if I tell you that you would receive a million dollars if you keep on thinking of that shirt for the rest of the day? You leave everything aside and focus only on that red shirt. You have a motivation to do so, a tangible benefit in the near future. This is how you have to act with quitting smoking, too. You have to motivate yourself with the belief that in the end you will only have gains. You won't receive a million dollars if you quit – well, depending on how much you smoke and might come to save that money – but you will gain something far more valuable: health, which is impossible to buy.

No matter how much money you might earn in life, it will not save you from dangerous diseases or illness. Once you quit, you will gain a new life, full of energy, you'll save money and you will gain the respect of those who believed in you. It won't be hard at all if you keep these goals in mind. On the contrary, you will take measures to quit more easily. Start being delighted and look forward to your new life.

People are more motivated to avoid pain and change, rather than seeking pleasure. Try associating pain with the non-fulfilment of your goals, so you may have your subconscious mind at hand more easily. It will then assist you to avoid the pain of failure and giving up. Change your mentality in such a way that if you fail and keep on smoking, you will feel more pain from the failure of giving in to rather than from withdrawal. Don't think about the act of smoking itself, but to the negative consequences that you will have to face if you give in to temptation. Offer yourself a small prize for each small victory; each time you overcome the symptoms of withdrawal, congratulate yourself.

There is a lot of information online that can help you enable your motivation. Listen or read other people's struggles, ideas, experiences and advice. This information will lead you towards your own goal. The techniques meant to motivate a person vary. Each person is different and reacts to different stimuli. Fill the future voids in your life with ways to enable your motivation or maintain it. It's a good way to distract yourself from cravings, while developing other aspects of your life.

Willpower is the ability to control your own thoughts and the way in which you behave (Cambridge Dictionary). **Willpower** is harder to control, especially if it isn't accompanied by motivation. It usually takes action when you don't receive and immediate reward, but in the foreseeable future. For instance, I got motivated lots of times to finish this book, but whenever my motivation wore off or it was clouded by negative thoughts, I used my willpower to finish it. In the case of willpower, the reward isn't yet tangible and we receive it later in life. For instance, you need willpower to go to school. I cannot imagine a person who is highly motivated to go, but, you know that, in time, school will outline your life. You may know this, but you still resist on going.

To start doing a task through willpower, you need to know that at some point you will be rewarded one way or another. Willpower, just like motivation, isn't an inexhaustible source and when you deplete it, it is difficult to resist cravings. You can keep willpower and "refuel its battery" in case you run out of it. To be able to keep willpower in storage for more important tasks, try not wasting it on insignificant tasks or decisions. For instance, if you don't want to take part in a certain event, well, simply don't. If you don't want to start a new project, one that isn't urgent, don't start it for the moment. Try focusing your willpower in these days on the struggle with nicotine cravings and withdrawal. I guarantee you that everything is worth postponing in this period. With the newly acquired energy from your life as a non-smoker you will be able to do them faster, and more efficiently. Willpower can be acquired through practice and it helps creating patterns in our mind in time. Once these patterns are formed, willpower will not be used to engage in any act. For instance, you don't need willpower to eat healthy; if you already eat healthy, you won't need any more willpower to resist the urge of smoking once you have resisted a few times. Willpower is the process of consciously integrating actions into our subconscious, until they turn into habits, patterns and ways of life. In other words, it turns into discipline in time through repetition. Use this information to integrate useful and beneficial actions into your subconscious. Practice makes perfect.

The subconscious knows it feels wonderful to lie in our bed all day and, thus, we have survived through life, even if we procrastinated, avoided tasks that seemed urgent. Therefore, we need the conscious mind to take action, for instance to make us do physical exercise. We know exercise does us well, but until we actually engage in it and make it part of our lives, and until we integrate it into our subconscious mind as an automatic process, we will use willpower to accomplish this task. While constantly repeating actions through willpower, we turn them into wishes. Think about the benefits of quitting smoking. Aim to quit smoking and any kind of nicotine consumption. Exercise the wish to quit as often as possible. Repeat to yourself: "I will quit smoking and I will enjoy my new life". The subconscious will adopt this autosuggestion and, shortly after, you will actually be eager to start this life's stage. This process doesn't take much time.

Do you feel like you don't have the willpower to perform any kind of physical exercise? I suggest you think again, remove useless habits like smoking and focus your willpower on exercising after you manage to quit. Paradoxically, you will have more willpower and you will feel more motivated after you exercise. Thus you will be charging your inner battery. Physical exercise releases lots of dopamine in a natural and healthy way, therefore helping you obtain it through other sources rather than nicotine. Moreover, exercise will also detoxify your body, making cravings less frequent and reducing withdrawal.

Try sleeping more, spoil yourself constructively. You need sleep, so we don't talk about postponing actions, but we talk about resting enough so you can feel powerful and able to confront any difficulties. Take care, though, not to spoil yourself with snacks and sweets. After you eat these, you'll feel guilty and this might weigh you down. It affects your motivation, it shakes your self-trust and image and you will feel the need for nicotine more intensely. Willpower can be affected also through a nutrient deficiency in our food, lack of vitamins and minerals. Their absence in the body creates fatigue, anxiety and even mild depression. Consult your doctor or a nutritionist to see if you lack any of these resources. Keep water handy so you don't get dehydrated. The brain needs lots of water to function properly. A brain that works at an efficient level produces the motivation and willpower necessary to carry out the tasks to the end.

Actually, make things easier for you and your future self. Your willpower reserves are limited, so throw yourself in progress-favourable situations. Plan events ahead, and how you will react to them. Are you going out? Where? Will you be tempted to smoke there? Yes. Then what measures can you take so you won't be tempted? Well, don't go. Or, if you need to go, don't take cigarettes with you, don't take money for cigarettes with you and don't stay in a group of smokers. If you do, ask them to help you by either not offering you cigarettes, or not letting you buy some for yourself. Plan ahead for any occasion that might occur, so you won't have to deplete your willpower and resist the temptations when they arise. Don't keep junk food or sugary beverages at home. It's easy to avoid them if you don't have them near you, and especially if you are not hungry or thirsty.

Discipline: training that makes people more willing to obey or more able to control themselves, often in the form of rules, and punishments if these are broken, or the behaviour produced by this training (Cambridge dictionary). In my point of view, discipline doesn't have any other "battery" than life itself and it comes into action when the "batteries" of motivation and willpower are depleted completely, but also when we have to fulfil routine tasks that are well printed in our instincts and psyche. In a way, it creates willpower and is created by willpower at the same time, but the two are separate phenomena. Discipline is actually the subconscious. In contrast to motivation and willpower, discipline is a set of rules. You don't need motivation or willpower to perform an act of discipline. Discipline can act in a conscious manner, but it resides in the subconscious. It is created by consciously taking action and, after a while, it will integrate itself in the subconscious through repetition. Once it lies there, the action will become instinctive, and thus, discipline is born, just like a reaction to triggers. The body is programmed to react to certain events, feelings, triggers. For example, it has to shiver when you are feeling cold to rise your body's temperature. It has to sweat when you are feeling hot, to cool you down. I am talking here about the basic codes in your genetic programming, the DNA, but also about mental processes and reactions to events that have been acquired throughout your life – like riding a bike.

Imagine you wake up and you find yourself next to a ferocious lion. If you are mature, you now it poses a threat. A toddler wouldn't really see the lion as a threat until it is thought (unless it growls, which would instinctively make the child unrest). Let's suppose we would meet an alien, one that looks nothing like with what we have seen so far. Our subconscious, through our eyes, will analyse it. It will notice its claws, sharp teeth and its size and will come up with a result, a reaction. The subconscious compares what we see, through the information and memory stored in our vast neuronal network, with the general information regarding claws (fear) + sharp teeth (fear) + big size (fear) and, disciplined as our mind is, will react through fright.

You should already have a general picture about what discipline is from a biological point of view. Let's see how we can consciously use discipline so that we may apply it to creating healthy and lasting routines into our psyche. Maybe it seems hard for you to act against your will. An illusion you might face here is that will is actually a masked subconscious pattern urging you to monotony. This is because conscious will is stimulated from the visual, tactile, olfactory and gustatory point of view. In short, if you are not used to eat broccoli, you won't like to eat vegetable, in spite of how much you consciously acknowledge the benefit of eating it. If you use your conscious willpower and eat broccoli repeatedly, I guarantee you that, in the end, you will end up liking it. The subconscious adapts to anything in life, and does it so easier when you leave negative thoughts aside. If you consciously block any attempt for something new, you will support your conservative subconscious mind. Anyway, if you try to quit smoking, as long as you do it with an open mind for change, and you are consciously willing to achieve this goal, the process of quitting will be easy. If you lock yourself up and despise the measures that need to be taken, it will be hard. Accept the inevitable and quit.

I understand that it is hard to do things forcefully -- until you get used to them and they are turned to discipline. Willpower alone is not enough sometimes; it can deplete after a busy day. Our tired mind fights a weak willpower and looks for treats by usually engaging in unhealthy activities. This is the subconscious' reaction to stressful situations. In time, you can train yourself no to fall in the trap of easy, harmful rewards when you are physically and mentally tired.

Don't worry. The process of training the "disciplinary muscle" is simple as long as you comply with a set of well-established rules. Write down a list of small, daily tasks that you can fulfill easily like: brushing your teeth twice a day, combing your hair before leaving your place, shaving, doing small physical exercise at certain hours, cleaning your shoes and so on. Follow these rules every day, whether you have time for them or not. The disciplinary muscle will thus strengthen and with it, your motivation and willpower reserves. By starting up with such simple tasks, you are improving your life, whilst learning to integrate disciplinary tasks into your subconscious.

The key to a disciplined life is to start off with small tasks, and later on intensifying them. Don't exaggerate! Propose realistic goals. I once read that a guy needed motivation to go the gym. So each day he would dress up, go to the gym, and walk away home. He continued repeating this process until he actually went inside and did some exercise. In time, he did more and more until the wish to go to the gym was natural. I am sure you can do better than this guy's start, but don't push it if you feel it's too much because you may end up quitting. Better safe and slow, rather than sorry.

Try associating these goals with results, even if they may seem "untouchable" at first. For instance, losing two pounds in a week can be really hard. Instead, try setting your goal to make more than usual exercise and to eat more balanced. The weight loss will soon follow after a while as a bonus to this action. This way, you will not get demotivated if you don't reach your goal in a predefined period of time. Your target should be action, then the results will either follow or not.

After you manage to integrate many small, beneficial tasks into your lifestyle and introduce some discipline, add extra tasks to your list. Establish new challenges each time a previous one transforms into discipline. You will not be able to jump from running two miles a day to running a marathon, but in time, "step by step", you will get there. Maybe this may seem discouraging at first, but think about it, if you don't take action at all, you don't accomplish anything. These small efforts will build up and, in time, you will realise things that you never thought that you were capable of. The truth is that you can throw yourself ahead into performing hard tasks, projects, and even succeed, but there is the same chance you can fail due to inconsistency and lack of discipline. Such a failure can deeply bring you down and will demotivate you to try further. This is why I recommend taking the small steps rather than exaggerations, failures or giving up.

Usually, sudden and radical lifestyle changes in a person, like suddenly quitting smoking as is the present case, could be results of a trauma: the loss of a beloved person, break-ups or life-breaking failures (i.e. missing out on opportunities that we can consider, in hindsight, to have changed the course of our life to a long desired goal. In the case of smoking, wasting a huge amount of money, health and other issues). These sudden traumas give us the impulse necessary to act and take control over our lives that have gone below the critical level. They wake us up to reality and ask for immediate measures to be taken, especially when they have irreversible physical effects upon ourselves. The subconscious struggles to take us out of that newly-imposed lifestyle and to rebalance our life, just like a person that doesn't know how to swim struggles in the water in order to catch a few breaths. If we don't want to go through this, then it is best to take care of our lives and be prepared for such eventualities. But how can we avoid such a situation? By taking notice in advance of the unpleasant possibilities that may occur in our life and shifting, consciously, our life until it tilts in the opposite direction. This can be done through discipline.

The idea of discipline is to do something that must be done whether you want to do it or not, in the absence of motivation and willpower. "Something seems impossible until it's done", said Nelson Mandela. Don't let yourself be fooled that it is impossible to quit smoking, that it is hard, that you don't have the necessary resources such as time, patience or energy. As long as you are alive, you can do anything you want provided you are disciplined enough. When motivation doesn't help you, activate your sense of discipline and work without seeking a resource or ambition to fuel you. You will succeed, and the fruit of your work will feed you for the rest of your life.

Motivation gives you the initial push, discipline urges you to go further. You might be motivated when starting up a new task, when you have an idea and are delighted to start it. But the motivation's reserves can deplete very fast, especially if you don't seem to get closer to your desired result, but rather further away. Discipline intervenes here, especially if you know the idea deserves a try. Usually motivation disappears when you start working; you notice that the task takes longer than expected and you lose your interest while saying: "I have done enough, I can continue another time." There usually isn't another time and you end up abandoning your project. If, at this moment, the task was overwhelming enough to make you stop, it will seem even hard later on when you try to start it again. A disciplined mind won't proceed this way. It will continue to work on the project without delay. Nothing is free in life; everything has a price. And the typical beneficial things in life have a higher price, whether it is paid in money or time. But for you to be able to accomplish something you have to invest these resources. Engage in action; don't give up on your path towards quitting smoking, like I haven't given up myself and others, too. We are now enjoying the benefits of a healthy life, and, finally, a peaceful life.

Take responsibilities over your life, actions and results. Claim this responsibility. Instead of blaming external factors for influencing it, instead of looking for excuses for not taking action, take responsibility for what you can do. Thus, you will influence your end results and life's events. If you have to go through a river, don't quit only because there is no bridge present, but build one or find another way to get on the other side. Don't sit still. Time is passing and life goes ahead, and so do you. You know that your target is on the other side of that river, so do everything that is possible to get there despite the difficulty. Don't blame external factors anymore; if you proceed this way, you admit that you are not capable of solving a problem. Is this true? Is there truly no other way to solve your problem? No, nothing is freely handed out to you, you have to accept the situation as it is and adapt to it, even dominate it. You have to use the resources you are able to control and it is not a sin to stop, but only after giving your best. You will notice that most things are, however, handy, one way or another, but you have to reach out for them or reveal the opportunities. If they aren't, you can find other solutions or improvise. You can beat a nail in wood with a stone; you don't necessarily need a hammer. It's harder, but you don't sit still, rather you find solutions and you'll succeed.

We seek to blame things that happen to us and that aren't under our control. We tend to accept less, to alleviate suffering, rather than fighting it off and seeking what we truly deserve. We look for excuses for the things we haven't done and we give up. Everything is under your control. You can quit smoking just by acting upon it, if you truly wish to quit, if you prepare and discipline yourself. There is no reason for postponing it, no factor to slow you down from living a healthy life. Think twice before lighting another cigarette up and ask yourself if you are pleased with living such a life of negligence only so that you don't endure a few symptoms of withdrawal.

To strengthen your discipline, consider yourself as already being a disciplined person, on the way of being even more disciplined. Don't think that you aren't disciplined, don't think that you are only trying to be. You already are and you want to be more. Discipline is one of the keys of successfully quitting smoking. You have to discipline yourself to attenuate withdrawals effects, even eliminate them, and simultaneously improving your life and organizing it. Discipline prepares you to favourably react to unpleasant events, to anticipate them and to act upon solving them. You will live a more fulfilling life through discipline, you will have more freedom and you will develop your ability to control your wishes.

We live under the illusion that we have to do what we enjoy and bring us happiness in life. This is what various "motivational speakers" are preaching, along lazy people who seek to justify their postponement. This is what our unambitious people around us teach. Then, we come to behave as such, acting like sloths. We should be educated to understand that this aspect of happiness is actually conditioned by multiple "layers" of reality. In short, lying in bed is comfy, it brings us joy and happiness, I admit, but if you were to stay all day in bed and wouldn't work at all, you wouldn't have a bed to lie on. You'd end up on the street. Thus, work does have to be a priority in life, and lying in bed is a reward. If you wish for more, do more. Even if the wish assumes pain through work, the final result is actually the goal and source of your present motivation and future happiness. Yes, maybe it is wonderful to eat junk food while watching shows; this is what really makes us happy, and we deserve a break from out daily routine. But if you come to think of it, is it really a break? Or are you eating unhealthy food throughout your day anyways? However, engaging in such activities only makes us happy for the moment. Later on we resume with a life in which we constantly blame ourselves for our physical appearance; we constantly lack willpower to resist such unhealthy behaviours, whilst damaging our psyche further with negative statements and feelings about ourselves. So, we end up accepting melancholy and guilt as part of our lives, as part of a means necessary to engage in unhealthy behaviour, instead of giving up these small pleasures for a greater good, for a more stable life, without appearance or behaviour complexes. Weigh down your decisions, and see if they offer you satisfaction on the long run, or they are just a temporary escape from your day's difficulties, escapes that might actually harm your future. In case you haven't noticed so far, I am mainly speaking about smoking here.

Evolve through discipline. You will like the process of disciplining yourself. It will integrate in your lifestyle before you might even think that it would be hard. Shortly after, you will notice the first signs of progress and, at a certain point, a better lifestyle is guaranteed.

THE FINAL PREPARATIONS FOR THE FINAL ATTEMPT

Together we have discovered how nicotine acts, what it is, how it uses our own bodies to create addiction, but also how we can use its own tricks against it. In this chapter, we are going to start our "battle plan". We will start the necessary preparations to confront nicotine, to attack it, and in the end defeat it. Now that you have identified all the means through which it manipulated you, it is like you have "stolen" its powers. It becomes more and more helpless and within this chapter we are going to hit it with a final blow.

You already know the fact that nicotine is removed entirely from your body after only a few days. But then, why do some people still feel the need to smoke months after quitting? The answer is based on a psychological level: they weren't ready to quit, in the first place, and after they did quit, nothing in their lifestyle (presumably) changed. They simply removed the cigarette from the equation, but they haven't built a new lifestyle, one of a non-smoker, to support their final decision. They didn't seek to replace the moments in which they smoked by doing something different, therefore those moments they associate with smoking keep coming back to haunt them.

They still stress when those moments arise and don't know what to do. Usually, lighting up a cigarette seems natural, but they can't anymore as they quit months ago. And still the void lingers in their gut. They never created a plan for a new lifestyle. An African proverb says: "If you want to move mountains tomorrow, you have to start by lifting stones today". Your ambition to quit is useless if you don't remove the obstacles in your path. Therefore, before quitting for good, you will remove these obstacles, namely creating positive changes in your life. Don't worry, they wouldn't be drastic changes, but are changes meant to help you adapt smoothly to your new life.

A problem that many people who buy motivational books face is that they expect statements and quotes that will, somehow, simply change their mindset and force them to action. It's like they expect the author to "snap" their fingers and suddenly the reader is cured of a lifelong problem. This doesn't work this way. We, the authors, are guides through your life, either showing or recommending you pathways for the better, but it is solely your choice and possibility to take action upon reading our words. We help lost wanderers find their path back to glory, but the wanderers (readers) themselves are the true heroes.

Anyways, don't expect to be instantly motivated to quit. This isn't how things work. In this book, various aspects regarding smoking and nicotine are presented to you, facts actually, but the sole decision to take action and quit must light up from your   own   spirit.

Anything that I would tell you, if you don't decide for yourself to quit, you won't succeed. You need your own reasons to quit, not simply the obvious ones: bad smell, fatigue, and wasted money as it isn't enough to rely solely on them. You will be unable to break the emotional bound you have with the cigarette. Smoking is an emotional behaviour, so the decision to quit must be emotional as well. The problem is not that you are too weak to quit, too addicted to stop, it simply is a hard process not related to either of the two reasons. The problem is that you didn't rely on emotions to declare a change in your life, in other words, you have never really wished, desired, longed to quit smoking. I know it isn't easy. Words at best written on a piece of paper won't help, but you aren't alone. Let's step further together, I'm here to help.

Starting now, you will prepare for the day in which you become a non-smoker. Physically and mentally. The physical part is rather easy, you resist nicotine consumption, of any kind, for a few days and the body will dishabituate from it. Your body can replace adrenaline with natural energizers by natural and healthy ways. The psychological part requires more work, especially if you aren't yet convinced to quit smoking. . I don't know if you have noticed, but my whole book is based on preparing yourself psychologically, emotionally. Even the biological chapter has its role to prove to your subconscious how dangerous tobacco is. Truly wish to quit smoking and allow your subconscious to process this information. Consciously integrate this info into your subconscious until it turns into a pattern of thinking.

REPLACING SMOKING WITH OTHER NICOTINE SOURCES

I don't recommend you use nicotine patches, sprays nor nicotine gum or other products that contain nicotine. They have been invented to offer you the illusion of freedom, while keeping you addicted to the main substance that causes all this fuss: nicotine itself. As you have already learned in the previous chapters, this substance is the biological factor that determines you to smoke. Even if, maybe, you get rid of the hand to mouth gesture of smoking with the help of these products, you will still feel nicotine cravings and you will try seeking it through other ways, maybe even through smoking. As long as you don't read just your mindset and don't free yourself from the illusion that smoking is ok, you will start smoking again. The best way to quit is doing it "by the book", as I have myself. In contrast to myself, you have the advantage of having all this information handed out to you. All the information I gathered and used is concentrated into this book, and all you have to do is read these words and understand meaning and, further, applying their essence to your life.

These replacements offer the body the

nicotine it needs. It won't "heal" you of smoking biologically. They don't change your perception towards cigarettes, rather they simply mask the problem, until you cut them off to. Then, the problem will resurface, as you still are nicotine deficient and you will most likely resort to cigarettes to quell these feelings. These replacements create an illusion of you quitting, when actually, they haven't really done anything. The problem isn't smoking itself, but the nicotine addiction. Admit it. You like smoking. Once you won't use the replacements, you will start smoking again, because you don't have any reason to quit tobacco and your body will long for nicotine anyways. The psychological desire to hold a cigarette in your hand doesn't disappear either, to exhale that smoke. Since these replacements don't offer us those moments in which we can disconnect from the world and smoke in peace and quiet, we may tend to smoke despite the nicotine patches, even if we will feel nausea from the nicotine overdose. This actually happened to me.

You will be firmly convinced that you will succeed. You don't have to infest your body with these replacement products. If you do use them, your mind will perceive this as a sign weakness and submission to nicotine. It intensifies your fear of quitting. You reaffirm to your subconscious that you are truly addicted to nicotine and that you are afraid to quit, you stall, wait for non-existing easy ways, and after you fail in your low quality attempts, the fear will amplify. It's like clinging with your last finger on a rock before falling off the cliff.

Not even electronic cigarettes are a solution. Leaving aside the fact that you are still considered a smoker, they are uncomfortable, they contain many toxins as well and even more nicotine as classical cigarettes – our main problem exactly. Then, I ask you, how can they be a solution to our issue? Many people smoke classical cigarettes, whilst smoking the electronic ones. It's obvious that the problem is far more complex, and deep down, you know this as well. Don't look for excuses and don't postpone quitting smoking with trying out other techniques. There is only one way to get rid of this vice, and that way is simply believing that you can and will.

You are strong and you don't need these replacements. Continue reading this book and you will convince yourself into quitting, on your own.

PSYCHOLOGICAL PREPARATION

Any action is determined by our thoughts and it begins with the firm decision of starting it, therefore we will begin to prepare psychologically first, and then physically. All that you have done in life, all that represents you as a person, all that you are now is owed to a set of decisions you have made in the past, either good or bad. Even not taking a decision is actually, in the end, a decision that has influenced your current personality. Now you will take the decision to improve your life and health, beginning with a small change in your perception upon reality.

A SMALL REPROGRAMMING OF THE BRAIN

You are stressed, you light a cigarette up to make you feel better, to relax. It's an escape. When you drink alcohol, you smoke so that you feel better, to amplify your state of relaxation. Actually, all destructive behaviours have this thing in common: they are generated by emotion which we don't even notice or can't even understand. You receive an emotional reward instantly, even if the actions itself is harmful. That is why, the need for pleasure is greater than the need to survive. Well actually, it isn't, but as long as the subconscious isn't aware of the damage you do whilst smoking, it won't consider it as such a danger.

How can you replace this? Each time you learn something new, the same reward area in your brain activates. Hereby, the brain releases dopamine and makes you feel happy, ambitious, proud, motivated. The most efficient way to stay happy without smoking is to learn something new about yourself while trying to quit, as you do now through reading these words. Personal development is the key to freeing yourself emotionally from cigarettes. Through it, you can stimulate dopamine production in your brain and get over addiction.

We will start with a small reprogramming of the brain through understanding a few hidden behaviours related to smoking. The source of each transformation is our own potential. As long as potential remains potential, no such transformation will occur. It isn't enough that we read about how to accomplish things, to gather information, we must also act upon them. This means, we have to express desire to quit smoking with the mind and heart open, so we may cultivate this potential.

Most smokers think that all that must be done to quit is to resist the urge of smoking until the cravings disappear. This is the hard way, because smoking, especially the hand to mouth gesture we associate with it, is just a small part of everything that happens. Each lit up cigarette is preceded by the thought of smoking, an emotional state. Thoughts affects our emotions, and the emotions affect our behaviour. For example, if you think you are weak, you will feel weak and you will emanate weakness in your behaviour. If you feel charismatic, you will behave charismatic and good things will shortly follow. While you are smoking you probably have positive thoughts such as: I feel good, I have more inspiration, cigarettes bring me great joy, I like the taste of burnt tobacco etc. These lead to positive emotions regarding smoking, emotions that encourage smoking. To quit smoking, you must first change what your mind thinks about smoking.

So, what happens in a smoker's mind a while after they quit? An internal dialogue is born that sounds like: "I want a cigarette. But it's not ok for me to smoke anymore. But I want a cigarette. But I can't smoke, I won't do it. Yet I still want a cigarette, it makes me happy".

Behold what happens when such a dialogue occurs:
1. The imagine inside your mind is that of a cigarette;
2. Your thoughts begin and end with a cigarette. Everything revolves around it.

If all you can think about is being unable to smoke that desired cigarette, you are creating an inner conflict. Your mind, your subconscious, actually, cannot process negative commands. For example, try NOT to think of a bride right now. Think of anything else, but definitely don't think of a bride. Try to resist... What are you thinking of? A bride. You create a sensation of endeavor that is overwhelming and, in the end, you surrender. The same happens when you fight the urge to smoke. You don't think of anything else but cigarettes. So, how can you change your mentality regarding your need of tobacco? The "battery" that fuels this internal dialogue is constituted by the words we use. They create images. Words create thoughts and words thus lead to action. These words will determine the way in which the mind and the body will feel the need for nicotine. Let's try another exercise. Imagine now you are biting into a lemon, watch out, don't swallow it. Imagine intensely how you are biting into that sour lemon. What happens? You didn't really bite into one, but yet you still feel the sourness. Your saliva seems to retreat and your buccinators muscles seem to contract from the sourness. Thoughts have affected your body. In the same way, when you either say the word cigarette or think about one, your mind will start revolving over this subject and provoke the effects you so wish to get rid of, like cravings. While these cravings thus intensify, you will think about the cigarette even more, thus making the cravings even stronger, until you give in and light one up. This is the power of suggestion and, as you already know, for the best results in life it is better to use it with positive thoughts and action. Did you ever notice sometimes that you might be relaxed, with no thoughts or need to smoke, and suddenly, you somehow remind yourself that you didn't smoke for a while? Suddenly, a huge craving and urge to smoke appears. If you did experience such a situation, and you probably did but never regarded it, then you may already know that these cravings occur more psychologically rather than biologically.

All you have to do is to replace the word "cigarette" with another word, for instance "air". You can't do this at one fling, but with practice. Instead of thinking that you want a cigarette, tell yourself that you want air. You need air. Breath in deeply, exhale and imagine that you have satisfied this desire. The mind will think that you offered it what it needs. . Do it as often as you need to, repeat it until it forms a pattern, and replaces your cravings for cigarettes. Your body asks, you give it what it wants. You won't feel as bad as after smoking, but more relaxed, more complacent, especially because in the end you did offer yourself what you wanted. And you can offer it this anytime it desires. As a bonus, you get to oxygenize your body through these breathing tricks, you receive energy to ward off further cravings and your mind will focus much easier on your tasks. The feeling of withdrawal will be totally different (if at all)and will pass much faster. Actually, you can use any word that resonates with you. The more often you use it, the easier it'll be to do the same thing next time, until it's done automatically. Hence, you are slowing replacing cravings for a cigarette with that for air. It becomes an automatism, like riding a bike. You can apply this technique to any vices or cravings, and you can even replace that word with an action. If you start thinking about cigarettes and feel the need to smoke, replace the need to smoke with the need to do physical exercise, on the spot. If your mind says, "I want to smoke", try changing that into "I want to exercise", all the while taking action until the craving eventually disappears. Tricking your own mind like this can be so simple. Just try it.

You create your own reality on what a cigarette means to you and your life. As long as you continue suggesting that you need it, that it offers you pleasure and joy, the subconscious will think so and take the information as such. Therefore, it will act as it has always in the absence of a cigarette: it will torment and nag you into smoking. As long as you let your mind believe that a cigarette will free you from anxiety and that it will ca you down, make you more sociable, you end up falling more and more into its trap and you will continue experiences cravings, therefore continuing to smoke. Indeed, it offers you all that you imagine it does, but you will never enjoy the benefit of living the life of a non-smoker, in which you can feel and have all that a cigarette provides, even more, including health.

THE REASON WE QUIT SMOKING

Now comes some advice that you might not heed to. I admit, I didn't listen to such advice myself while I read it in other books or when motivational speakers urged me to do so. But only because, for example, I was asked to establish a final goal in my life, and to write the steps necessary to get there. I find it really impractical, unrealistic. In most cases, you need money to progress in these goals and to be able to take the next steps towards them. You need money to travel the world, to do business or even to put your life in order, to pay your debt.

Most of these, and many more examples, depend on money, a factor that we might not be able to influence. If money is not the issue, then maybe your social status, connections. Yes, you might be able to build relations and climb on the social ladder, but is the hassle really worth it? It does if it gets you to your dream goal, but a life of seeking happiness could be a miserable life. You may spend most of it seeking a distant pleasure, instead of enjoying what could be in your grasp. Maybe it does work for some, but I don't consider simply writing the steps down enough. In my opinion, getting your life into order and perfecting each aspect slowly, but progressively, is more important. Consolidating what you have, what skills you possess and then slowly acquiring new talents is a much easier way for you to reach your goals, rather than relying on a fixed plan on how to get there. This may blind you from other opportunities, ironically distancing you from the goal. Anyways, we are currently doing something important and tangible. We are setting a goal that has instant rewards and can be obtained immediately. So, to reach it, you have to compose a list of your own personal reasons to quit smoking. Don't write vague reasons, get into details. Some vague reasons for you to quit would be for the money, the savings. Some detailed reasons is that because you waste money on smoking, you are missing out on things, like going out more often with your friends or loved ones, buying new clothes more often or other things you might wish for.

Write the list down on your device, or on a piece of paper. Keep it handy and constantly add reasons to it as soon as you come up with one.

Don't forget to get into details, in order have the real feel of the reasons each time you read them. It's important that you start building this list right now, so that it is long enough and ready when you need it most. You might think you are able to remember all these reasons, but when you need them most you won't remember all of them, or at least not in detail. Eventually if you don't like creating lists, write a long text about how you conceive a perfect life for yourself, as a non-smoker, and try aspiring to that. Include the benefits of a non-smokers life into that text.

Use a positive tone to come up with the list, avoid negatives. Don't write things like: "I can't afford new shoes", rather write "With the savings from quitting, I will afford to buy a new pair of shoes per month". Investing a small amount of time into creating this list now will give you a thrive later on, when you go through withdrawal and temptations to smoke.

Maybe money isn't an issue for you. Maybe you don't really smoke a lot and you afford wasting money on cigarettes. But is it really so? You would surely afford a bit of extra luxury by quitting, at least in health. As I said earlier in this book, smoking slows you down and creates brain fog. This means that while you waste money on smoking, your productivity suffers, making you less efficient in life, in business or at your work. Calculate how much money you spend on cigarettes per month and write it down on your list. Either big or small, you will undisputedly raise your quality of life through the savings. Think about how you could spend those savings each month. Maybe there are enough for a simple therapeutic massage per month, but maybe if you add it up, you could afford to travel once a year to new places.

Compare the money you spend on cigarettes with the price of the things you don't possess and wish for. You will notice that you would live a better life if you would spend it on something better. You try really hard to save money or you work really hard for money, while you could simply have the extra money without the hassle, stress and effort by simply quitting. In time, you might be able to afford a new phone, a vacation or even a new car. You don't go out with your loved one as often as you would like, you don't buy her flowers, but when it comes to smoking you spend even your last cents for a pack. I am not scolding you, but think about how unhealthy smoking is to your life solely from this point of view. Calculate how much money you have spent on cigarettes since you started, and how much money you would have had now if you had saved the money. You can't recover that money now, put you can prevent looking back 10 years from now and facing the same problem.

I admit, I feel that I have lost a good part of my childhood and youth with smoking. This may sound dramatic, but if I would have never smoked in the first place, I would have had more money, better clothes and gadgets, or I would have travelled more often. Life would have been different, richer, colorful and fun. I would have spoiled myself more often, I would have had energy to work out and have the body I always desired. But I continued smoking instead. And to what end? I was neither more energetic, rich, smart or relaxed. All I did was waste myself and my past years. Whenever I would think of this, I would try to justify the reasons I smoked before, but all in vain. There exist no real justifications to smoking, only your own weakness to resist temptation. Anything a smoker gains through smoking, a non-smoker has too, even more. Think about yourself. Maybe you find yourself in these words. In exchange to all you could have had and could have been, you chose to continue smoking. When you understand this, anxiety might fall down upon you and you might think that it is futile to stop now since you have been smoking for so long and have already wasted so much. You will be spiteful that you lost so much, that you can't do anything to recover everything you "burned" so far with the cigarettes. This spite may seem to stop you from progressing and quitting right now, you feel that, if you would admit this waste, you would give it further "life", you would admit your past mistakes of smoking, you make it feel more real. You don't want to confront the realities of the past and the things you have missed out on or could have done better in your life, as a non-smoker. You can't, and you don't want to, imagine the life you could have had if you never started smoking in the first place. However, the time has come for you to face this issue, to face your past. Don't let yourself be overwhelmed by hate, but reconcile with what has been, and embrace what can be from now on, what you can turn into, what you can create with a new life.

It is never too late to be the person you could have been. You may think now that if you quit smoking now, your whole "investment" in smoking, your past even, becomes irrelevant. You may feel like admitting your past failures. So you might be tempted to continue smoking, rather than assuming responsibility. Take care, you will end up blocking yourself again and rejecting any progress or positive change in your life. The mind won't allow you to hurt yourself this way, so it will consider that it is better for you to continue smoking rather than admitting you were wrong. You will continue being a prisoner to cigarettes and you will regret later on in life that you didn't quit.

You don't have to think that you have wasted your life and lost everything. Rise from the ashes of your cigarettes like a "Phoenix" and you will achieve more than you can ever imagine and even more than you would have achieved if you have lived your entire life as a non-smoker, possibly monotone. Now you may have an advantage. Through the newly acquired knowledge in this book, a fire might start burning inside of you that might propel you to recover all that has been lost so far. This fire, this boost in ambition and willpower, will help you thrive and reclaim the life you should have had. You probably already have a beautiful life to begin with, whether you realise it or not, the simple fact that you are alive is a blessing. In the end, all you need to succeed in life and to fulfil your goals is the ability to think and breathe. Positive changes in life can happen from one day to another, and you should be prepared, be at your best level, to embrace them. Cigarettes might have slow you down so far from your goals, but you are still on course. They might have repressed your potential, but once you quit for good, you can do much more, especially with the new flame burning inside yourself. Smoking might have cut some of your possibilities so far, but it doesn't matter anymore, since there might be more to come. Don't live in the past, rather live in the present. Be proud of who you are and think about what you are prepared to be.

It is impossible to literally recover all the time and money you have wasted on smoking, but you can recover it in another way: grant more attention to life. Don't let it pass by uncontrolled, like you have let it pass so far. Fight your inner demons, be stronger than them, and more conscious to the value of life. Thus, even if you missed the start to a non-smoker, the power you acquire once you transform into a non-smoker and the incredible ambition along, will push you. You will recover everything you thought has been lost, regardless of your age. Maybe you might even receive a bonus, a stronger boost, that a non-smoker, who didn't go through the trauma of realising what has been lost in life so far, doesn't enjoy. You are going through this trauma and will learn to value life even more while giving more regarding to the beautiful things that are happening around you, in your life. You will live fully. You will do more exercise, with more energy and vigor. You will be more careful with your friends, your family, your love. Now, that you have more time and energy, you can do all these things, even more, because you are actively conscious.

The truth is that we often try to quit smoking not because we got bored of it but because other factors occur like the lack of money, health or that we feel compelled to do so by a person. Because of these reasons, a lot of individuals fail. They don't really wish to quit smoking and they feel that they are sacrificing their source of joy and pleasure for an external factor. Withdrawal starts and the fact that they cannot smoke anymore is making them unhappy. They didn't really want to quit, they were obliged to do so. The result in this case is relapse and the neglection of the real reasons they should quit.

We hear stories of people that try to quit smoking by other peoples impulse. Some might succeed, but they still yearn for the "good old days" in which they were smoking. This yearning can last, in this case, for a lifetime. They have simply removed the biological addiction, but not the psychological one. They didn't "heal" themselves completely. They lead a life of suffering and longing for cigarettes. I bet that after reading all of this, you aren't really encouraged to quit. Maybe you manage to get over the biological addiction, but you feel incomplete and what to continue smoking to quell the psychological cravings. This is why you actually have to wish to quit smoking. The hardest part in quitting is the psychological addiction, not the biological one. In this case, the most important reason to quit is to do so for yourself. You want a change in good. You want health, money, balance in life, physical exercise and the energy to solve real problems in life.

Try working on the earlier mentioned list right now. Or at least start it now. You will need it later on. It's possible you might even learn new things about yourself while completing the list. Hidden desires and longing that were deep down in your subconscious might be revealed. You will have the opportunity to fulfil those too.

WILL IT BE HARD TO QUIT?

It will only be hard if you allow it to be hard. Now that you understand what happens in your body and in your mind, what factors generate these cravings for nicotine and why withdrawal can sometimes be unbearable, you will be able to use the information to make the process of quitting smooth. The simple solution to withdrawal is that when you feel it is getting hard to abstain, you find other preoccupations to distract your attention. Don't let yourself be overwhelmed by thoughts about cigarettes. Once you distract your mind with other things, you will notice immediately that the stress is rather psychological. You don't actually need cigarettes. Your body has not be designed to require them like it needs air, water, food, vitamin, but nicotine has the ability to fool you and create an illusion of need. We create the need ourselves, our mind simply reacts to it until thought otherwise. Our mind finds various reasons to make us continue smoking, and as long as we allow it to pursue these ideas it the longer the cravings last. Keep your mind and your life busy. Go to a theatre, to the cinema, opera or other places where you can not smoke. This way, you distract your mind while being unable to smoke. It is impossible to light up a cigarette in those places, and your mind does know this so it will not initiate cravings. Furthermore you have the opportunity to expand your cultural knowledge. Don't think continuously about the fact that you quit smoking, rather use the time to think about the benefits of quitting. Use your list. It is better to replace negative thoughts like being unable to relax with achievements: you have more money, you are healthier, you have more energy.

In the end, if you respect all the steps and measures needed to quit smoking that are suggested in this book, it won't be hard at all to quit. If, however, it will be, check if you truly are respecting all the ideas presented here and if you are truly trying to abstain from smoking, if you truly want to. Think that soon enough you will rid yourself of cigarettes and all this pain and your life will flourish.

PHYSICAL PREPARATIONS

Psychological preparation cannot be easy, especially if it is not accompanied by physical preparations. Now that you are psychologically prepared to quit smoking for good, or while you are still working on it, we can start the physical preparations. They consist in a few things that you can start doing right now, even if you are reading this book for the first time and you are probably still smoking. You don't have to do everything only once you quit. Some things can be dealt with right now, so once you are a fresh non-smoker you will be able to confront other issues. Once you quit tobacco, other various symptoms might appear. They won't let you think clearly and your mind will try to convince you to continue smoking. That is why a physical preparation that is done in time, slowly until you get used to the small changes and the new lifestyle as a non-smoker, will be of great help. We will try to decrease withdrawal symptoms as much as possible and we will try to remove all triggers that remind you of cigarettes and the fact of smoking.

REMOVING THE TRIGGERS

Smoking is toxic, dangerous and very hard to stop especially if you don't take the necessary measures to do so. It would be ideal if you don't experience any withdrawal. This is possible by removing the triggers, the objects and situations that remind you of cigarettes, of smoking. The main triggers are the cigarettes themselves. So try from now on, while reading this book and preparing for the future days, to smoke as little as possible. Reduce the number of cigarettes that you smoke. Actually try smoking just as much necessary for you to maintain your focus on reading this book. You will find that most cigarettes you smoked per day were unnecessary, without actually cravings. Rather they were smoked more out of boredom, habit or to fill the voids, the moments in your life in which you have nothing else to do. Try smoking less cigarettes and try to stop smoking in places you typically did so – on the balcony, at home, on the street, in the car.

Avoid any situations that may provide triggers to smoke. It is hard, but not impossible. Our lives gravitate around custom events and daily activities, routines. We have a schedule and most actions of what we do daily are already printed inside our subconscious, alongside the need to smoke while performing these actions. Our social circle is already formed. It probably contains some smokers, events and occasions to smoke happen anyway, like cigarette breaks. Some events might provide stress, others might make us want to smoke without us even realising it. When going to such events, try simply taking less cigarettes with yourself, three or four should suffice if you would usually smoke a pack. Or even try not taking any cigarettes with you, and abstain from buying a new pack. You can remind yourself that you are allowed to smoke once you get back. If you typically smoke while talking on the phone, try going to a place where you can't smoke while doing so and you don't have any access to cigarettes. Try drawing while talking on the phone instead of smoking. There are many adult colouring books – lots of people claim it helps reduce stress to draw or colour in such books. Buy pens, paper and such books and keep them handy you don't get tempted to smoke while on the phone.

The need to smoke can manifest itself through a feeling of emptiness in your stomach, similarly to the feeling of hunger. Keep nuts, unroasted peanuts, carrots or any other healthy, non-fattening, food at hand. Chew sugar-free, mint flavoured, gum. Mint represses the need to smoke. Dispose of any junk food inventories you might have. Throw them out now, or give them away at least and abstain in buying such food in the future, otherwise the reasons you will gain weight from quitting is not the fact that you quit, rather the extra junk food you eat to distract yourself from smoking. Junk food releases dopamine and once you get rid of your nicotine addiction, a new one could follow through it. Typically, you feel the need to eat something salty, not junk food per se, but unhealthy food is always easier to acquire or at hand. So it is better to keep salty foods at hand like cheese or nuts. Once your metabolism temporarily slows down from quitting smoking you don't want to find yourself surrounded by unhealthy food that could diminish your overall health.

After about five to six days of quitting you will surely feel much better. Think of the situation. Will your loved ones be proud of yourself? Without doubt. This could fuel you to continue. Are cravings as bad as before? Of course not. They weaken with every moment you resist them. Don't you feel more dynamic knowing that you have done something great in your life, worthy of admiration, something that not many people can praise about? Do you feel more energy? More vigor? Do you notice significant, positive, changes in your life? Write these changes down and read them each time a trigger to smoke might occur. Your life surely has bettered itself, but you can't notice it because you are constantly bombarded by your subconscious with reasons to continue smoking. Even if you didn't achieve much so far, the simple fact that you quit smoking, save money and improve your health is a victory. Your body becomes healthier with each second, minute, hour and day that passes, so don't get discouraged. Cleary achievements exist, you just have to notice them.

Repeat in your mind slogans like: "I am not poisoning myself, I am stronger and great things await" each time cravings amplify. It might sound ridiculous to keep repeating such motivational and inspiring texts, but as you have learned so far, they do affect your subconscious as much as someone would tell you that you have gained weight. Whether you want it or not, you will remember these phrases for a while. Motivational quotes encourage you to become a better, healthier, person. They help you admit the possibility of change while stimulating the fight against tobacco. Affirm as much as possible your desire to succeed, to quit. Tell your friends occasionally about what you are trying to achieve, about your progress so far and ask them to help you by not offering you any cigarettes and ask them to try not smoking around you. They will surely encourage you, and the pride you feel when you show them that you can quit will strengthen your cause of quitting. You can be stronger with their help.

Another typical trigger is food. Sometimes we smoke after eating because we have the impression that cigarettes offer us please, satisfaction and relief if we ate too much. A cigarette after a plentiful meal is sometimes heaven on earth. It makes us appreciate and fully savour food. With this in mind, we do not notice thought that it actually destroys our sense of smell and taste, making us actually feel the pleasures brought by food, less. We can't fully savour a meal, not even the presence of the people surround us while eating, because we can barely wait to finish eating and light a cigarette up afterwards. I am surely you can relate to this and notice this type of behaviour in other situations as well. How many joys in life are you passing away only so you are able to smoke? You always wait for something beautiful to end so you can go out and smoke. In this case, simply stop eating too much and don't put yourself in the situation of feeling like you are about to explode. This makes you crave for a cigarette to relieve that feeling of over-satiety. Remind yourself that after you eat you don't smoke to savour the food, rather you smoke because you are simply addicted.

Fear, anxiety and panic are smoke-triggers as well. In principle, when you panic, you have to breath more often and deeply to calm down, yet smokers prefer to light a cigarette up which makes this impossible. They get fooled by the adrenaline produced while smoking and the calmness provided by the lack of oxygen in our brain, by the pleasure of dopamine release. Thus, all these make you forget about the initial reason you had a panic attack, while the real threat still exists, unapproached and unsolved, waiting to surface once more once you are relieved by the symptoms caused from smoking. A new illusion.

The mere fact of knowing that you ran out of cigarettes can produce fear or a new panic attack, as you might have already experienced on your own skin. Once you turn into a non-smoker, the fear that you have to change your daily routine, which presently includes smoking, can appear. This can also urge you to continue smoking. Trust me, you will adapt to a new lifestyle, a smoke free routine.

Others could, you can as well .It's not the event itself that terrifies you, but the fear that you can't handle it without cigarettes. You have to have more trust in yourself. You are a wonderful, strong being that can handle any challenges, as long as you believe in yourself. Anyways, you should avoid any triggering events, at least in the beginning stage of your new, smoke-free, life. Some missed out social events now will bring out many benefits in the future.

In the earlier subchapters *Caffeine* and *Alcohol* I have explained that these trigger the need to smoke. Try avoiding them for a while, until you are fully adapted to your new lifestyle and sure about them not causing you any cravings. If you can't abstain from them, try at least consuming them in places where you can't smoke, try not having any cigarettes, or the possibility to buy them, available.

Avoid getting bored. Sometimes boredom might trigger a craving. While working, your mind has other concerns instead of nagging you to smoke. When you don't have any activity, it will try to determine you to smoke to fill those voids in time. Try reading in those moments. Sink in to a story of a book until an opportunity to do something else arises. Don't let your mind wander off, especially in the beginning phase of your new lifestyle. It could trick you into smoking or cause you enough paint to give in. Watch inspiring online videos, call someone, do some exercise, try sleeping or mediating in your free time.

I am pretty sure you have a lot of lighters and ashtray either at your home or at your workplace. Get rid of them so it will be harder for you to smoke. You shouldn't be smoking at home or at your workplace anyway, because you have to remove any smell soaked into the walls, clothes, curtains. These smells could also be triggers to smoking in the future. The subconscious can feel it certainly and it will remind itself that it didn't urge you to smoke lately. Wash all your cloths, curtains and eventually you can use anti-tobacco sprays.

Did you notice how sometimes a lot of time passes and you didn't have any urge to smoke? You felt well and all was fine. Then suddenly, you are somehow reminded that you didn't smoke for quite a while and it would be a good time to light one up. At that moment, especially if you don't have any cigarettes handy, your mind and body go crazy. You start experiencing hard cravings, think about smoking constantly and seek for ways to smoke. But a few seconds earlier, all was fine. You start trembling and getting dizzy. This is clear proof that you are addicted more psychologically rather than physically. A notorious smoking-trigger is your own mind. It's pretty hard to master it and you can defiantly not get rid of it, but you can convince it that you don't need any cigarettes. You can try the earlier mentioned technique, the one with replacing tobacco cravings with air cravings. It worked for me, it worked for other readers, it will surely work for you too.

Think about what other triggers you may have and try removing them within the limits of possibilities. Analyse and eliminate them until your first day as a non-smoker or at least create an action plan on how to handle them when they arise. Be careful not to create new triggers though, in example, if you start meditating, don't do it while smoking. You may create a new link, an association, between those two actions that could trigger a need for smoking while meditating when you are a non-smoker.

DOPAMINE SOURCES

I have talked about dopamine in a previous chapter. As you already know, it is a main cause for your smoking habit and it creates a high level of addiction. You have to find new, healthy and natural, ways for your body to release dopamine into your brain. Currently, as a smoker, your dopamine receptors are affected and the dopamine you should receive from little things is insignificant. You need stronger stimulants to feel its effects. How will you adjust your dopamine concentration? How can you get your dopamine needs back to normal levels? The first step to take here is to quit smoking completely and in time the dopamine receptors will heal themselves. After a while, you will start enjoying the little things in life that you currently are unaware of. This way, even giving or receiving a small compliment will make you just as happy as smoking a cigarette, but give it time. Have realistic expectations. Smoking is the leading cause of, preventable, death, a serious issue. You can't expect everything to turn out fine just by snapping your fingers, but you can expect for the to turn out just great by acknowledging the reality and accepting the facts.

When you start enjoying the little things in life more, it means that your dopamine receptors are healed and they will continue to work properly. If you allow nicotine to cloud your judgement and have resentments over the fact that you quit, you will continue ignoring the little things in life and you will have to endure withdrawal. If you can't find joy in the life you have, you will find pain in seeking it. Like any precious thing, the mind needs time to heal. Don't get discouraged at the beginning if things don't work out as you may have imagined. You have just found out all this new information in this book, and you barely started acting upon them. Practice makes perfect. Time supports you. Simply offer your mind and body time to heal. "Massage" your dopamine receptors while actively enjoying little things like a smile, a blooming flower or the sun tickling you face, be happy to be alive.

Once you quit smoking, you will cancel out a dopamine source – nicotine. Without the usual flow of dopamine provided by it, you will feel demotivated. The little things that can stimulate dopamine production in a non-smoker will not work for you, momentary. That is why, until you actually quit for good, you should try receiving dopamine from other sources. It is important you start healing those dopamine receptors right now. Prepare before quitting, start enjoying and valuing the things that surround you. This way you will be able to face the lack of nicotine and it's side effects. I will give you a list of dopamine sources you can use to facilitate the healing process of the receptors. None of the ideas from the following list harms your health, so you won't get hurt if you try some out:

• Enjoy the little things, actively, consciously. Watch as the birds fly and feel their freedom. Imagine that you are as free as they are, try emphasizing with them. Gaze to the beautiful blue sky and imagine what an endless world there is out there. Look at how the leaves dance on their way down when falling from a tree, feel and enjoy how the sunlight tickles your skin. Relax and observe the beauty of life and the fact that you are part of it'

• Learn something new. When we learn something new or understand something, the brain releases dopamine. Even in the moment you connect two pieces of information, the brain rewards you with dopamine

• Create something new. When, for example, we relax ourselves through an act of artistic creation, painting or sculpting, we receive dopamine;

- Listen to music. But only positive and uplifting music, not hate, anger or sorrow filled music. Listen to music in which you find yourself, filled with love, inspiration and pleasant vibes;

- Meditating, praying and self-reflection raise the dopamine levels inside our body. Think positive thoughts, not negative ones. Be grateful to the fact that you exist, to the fact that you are such a complex being. Think about how much joy you bring to those around you through your existence, because, whether you realise it or not, you mean a lot to at least one person. We are pressed by stress and frustrating activities daily. We work a lot and we don't make time to ponder upon ourselves. We don't truly know who we are, because we never made time to learn about ourselves. Sometimes we seem strangers even in our own eyes. We let ourselves be led by bad feelings and it seems that we give them more attention than they deserve. We have thoughts of anger, negativity, frustration and envy. Meditate or self-reflect, listen to yourself, your inner needs, your inner child that needs attention and provide it.

Try detoxifying your body. Help it remove nicotine and other toxins from your system. In the meantime, a detox can boost dopamine production because the toxins found in tobacco products inhibit the production and hurt the dopamine receptors. You can simply start by adding a few changes to your diet. Add tea or other natural remedies, take a few good naps, remove fatty products and sugar.

- Choose healthy food: dark chocolate, almonds, avocados, bananas, broccoli, carrots, peppers and protein rich foods. No, they aren't very tasty but you don't have to eat them all at once, you just have to progressively include them to your diet while removing other, unhealthy foods. Over time you will get used to them and you might even start enjoying eating such foods. They contain many nutrients that your body needs for its daily efficient functioning. Collaterally, their consumption will release dopamine. At a daily level, the body and the brain need certain nourishing substances for them to function properly and to survive. These are found in the above mentioned foods, and many others. We tend to avoid adding them to our diet, fact which leads to an unhealthy lifestyle. Then we come to judge our life and regard it as bad, slow, sad and hard. Simple modifications, like in your diet, can create the life you have always longed for, but your unhealthy behaviours cloud this opportunity. Ironically, we avoid almost everything that is healthy and good for us;
- Try to get enough rest. Don't deprive yourself of sleep, otherwise, your brain won't release dopamine easily and you won't be able to think clearly while fighting against nicotine. Try to

notice the reasons why you don't sleep enough and try reorganizing your time. Sleeping an extra hour can give you many more hours of productivity per day;

- Write down lists of what you have to do daily to optimize your life. Try adding only small tasks at first, that you can always, easily, manage and check them each time you finish one. You will see that your efficiency rises when you create a long list and start checking tasks out. Your brain will reward you for each item on the list with dopamine. Write on that list tasks like: organizing your drawer, your desktop (physical and digital), 5 minute abs, call your parents (especially if you haven't talked to them for a while) – knowing that you have made them happy with your call will give you a dopamine boost. Offer your loved one flowers or a small gift. Write down your own ideas and create such a list. Try adding tasks that bring joy to others as well, this will improve your social life in the meantime. Make the list longer, but only with easy and realistic goals, otherwise you will feel overwhelmed. You can plan ahead for a whole week. The gain will be double: you receive dopamine through other sources than nicotine and you complete little tasks that make your life better. We tend to focus too much on major tasks, and we might not even be able to finish them because we feel overwhelmed. This can lead us to enter a state of anxiety which will further slow us down. We tend to ignore all the little improvements we can bring to our life. These improvements can make our life feel just as enjoyable as would major ones, but we are taught to focus on what society dictates we should. "Start your engine" with these small tasks so you can receive motivation through dopamine and so that you can have the drive to face and finish the bigger challenges with more ease. If you start working on the harder tasks, and you don't manage to finish them, you might become cynical, depressed, demotivated. You might lose your self-confidence if you engage in complex activities that you cannot end or in which you don't feel any progress, unless you have a small list of finished achievements behind;

- A little trick I personally use to facilitate dopamine release is to close my eyes and to think about something pleasant or a past achievement in life of which I am proud. I try re-living that moment of glory, hence I manage to generate a small amount of dopamine. Think about your first kiss, about how you manage to finish a challenge, of how other praised you for your work or achievements, or try thinking about any event that brought joy to your life and made you the person you are today.

In principle, engagement in any activity that brings you joy. Start working on this list right now, and don't neglect it in the future days.

Keep it at hand and whenever you feel you have nothing to do, and you notice you are urged to smoke, check a task from the list. Try acting upon the list as often as possible, even when you are not bored. Dopamine is pleasant and you can make use of it at any time.

In my opinion, the best dopamine sources, the most constant and pleasant ones, are enjoying the little things in life. Once you heal your dopamine receptors you will find it easy to do so. Just be open to them, admit the joy you receive from even a soft touch. Learn to be happy about life as it is right now. If you feel it is not enough, be happy anyways, as long as you can breath and as long as you are willing to take action, change for the better is prone to come, just believe in yourself and what you can achieve. Everyone has been born the same, but only few use their main trump brought from life, the ability to create – so create, stop judging what has been in your life, and start acting for a better one.

I know it is hard to do all these things I mentioned, even to create the list. Maybe you won't even do it, but I urge you to try at least some things out even if you are sceptical. You will then see and feel what I am talking about. You will see that you will start feeling much better and you might even get addicted to self-progress. This doesn't sound too bad, and trying to reach this positive addiction doesn't even require much effort. Focusing on little tasks, and finishing them, can motivate you to approach the more challenging ones. You can read this chapter any time again, if you don't feel prepared to act now, although, for the maximum effect, I strongly recommend you do so now. Otherwise, you might end up procrastinating instead of progressing. Receiving more dopamine through these methods will increase your mental acuity, focus, information processing and mood. Ironically, these are the things we seek to receive through cigarettes. Interesting, isn't it? What does this mean? Yes, a cigarette might provide dopamine through its perverse process, a process that distracts our attention from the joys we could receive through appreciating the little things in life while destroying our health. But if you CAN receive it through healthier ways and have the same effect, why not try it out?

If you replace cigarettes with the activities from the list I suggested you should create, you might even handle life easier and better than a person who has never smoked before does. Because, you see, you will be much more careful and you will seek satisfaction from more things through the process of replacing the false sense of joy received from burnt tobacco. You can stimulate dopamine production through the simple act of thought. Positive, uplifting thoughts. The mere idea that everything goes well in your life and that you are doing well so far, especially through reading this book and accepting the information within it, can increase your mood. Now, that you strive hard to quit smoking your brain will start supporting you with dopamine and you will be motivated to go through with quitting, but only if you embrace reality and accept the gravity if you continue smoking. Embrace reality, embrace change and soon enough you will embrace the life that you have always wished for. Be proud of yourself for coming so far and don't give up. Push forward and attack the nicotine problem with everything you have at hand. Since you have managed to read the book so far it is clear, that deep down in your soul, you desire change. This doesn't simply mean freedom from nicotine; this change will change the very foundations of your life and will reorganize it on many levels. Push forward and you will succeed.

PHYSICAL EXERCISE

When you engage in physical exercise, through sweat, you quickly eliminate nicotine and other toxins from the body. Through physical exercise will you, not only, adopt a new and healthy lifestyle, but you will also occupy your time, distracting your mind from cravings. Most books on helping you quit smoking don't really talk about this topic, I honestly don't know why. It is sure that you "shoot two rabbits with one bullet", maybe even more, at a time. Through physical exercise you get healthier, more vigorous, more active, intellectually agile and you will get into shape, thus increasing your self-confidence. You don't smoke while working out, and at the end, for a few hours, you won't feel the need to do so. Your fatigue decreases while your blood will get oxygenated and your lungs will function better.

Do physical exercise regularly. Any extra movement you do is a bonus compared to how much you are doing right now and it will help you get rid of nicotine addiction and withdrawal. Aside from removing nicotine from the body and encouraging your dopamine receptors to heal your general health increases while adopting a new hobby to keep you distracted from smoking. Be creative and get involved in exercise. Physical activity is an important instrument in quitting smoking. You can also use this to stimulate your metabolism that might slow down when quitting (only at the beginning), you stimulate your spiritual health, and in the end you will receive dopamine as a reward which will help you confront nicotine addiction and free yourself from its shackles.

Try exercising, but don't exaggerate if you are not used to it. Otherwise you might feel overwhelmed and tired and you might quit as fast as you started. Start with including small exercises into your daily routine, until you get used to them. It is important you do anything that is extra from what you are doing right now. If you don't have a favourite sport, now would be the best time to find one. I personally consider that going to the gym is the easiest and most efficient way of integrating physical exercise to your lifestyle. If you don't want to lift weights, simply use the treadmill or cycle. I recommend that you start searching for a gym, preferably close to your home, right now. Go to it and create a subscription, once you do this you have an extra reason to go. You could also try jogging, but as I said, it is way easier to start off at the gym. Jogging is a bit harder to start and you are not bound to continue it by a subscription or a personal trainer. Try the treadmill for now so you may "break the ice" now, not while in withdrawal and while your motivation may plummet. Either run on the treadmill or walk at a fast pace for at least 30 minutes. Slow and steady, but a sure progress to your health and daily routine. Remember not to overburden yourself with exercise in the first few days. You want to come to enjoy the activity, not dread it. Just work out long enough so you can be proud of the positive change you have brought in your life. All that really matters is adopting this healthy new lifestyle and eliminating the toxins and nicotine from your body so you won't feel withdrawal once you quit. Later on, you can do more exercise if you like. The cravings to smoke will reduce drastically. Exercising is a good way to overcome future afternoons in which you get back from work and you don't have anything else to do. Exercise so your mind won't be bored and tempted to induce cravings.

On the up side, you can also watch motivational videos while you run on the treadmill or listen to educational audio books. While working out and improving your health, you will also expand your knowledge and prepare for the next step in your glorious life as a non-smoker. This way you might even find a new hobby or interest in a subject that you can adopt later on.

I recommend you do exercise in the afternoon or in the evening, after work. Exercising in the morning is also good but we are currently focusing on stopping your cravings and in the morning you are busy with work anyways. It might seem exhausting to work out after work, but only the first few times. After a few tries, you would get used to it, even start loving the extra workout that will surely energize and motivate you. I guarantee that your brain will reward you with dopamine after engaging in such activity and it will stimulate you to do more. As I said, any beneficial activity that you do is rewarded by the brain.

If you exercise in the evening, after you finish it will get late. I can assure you that after any workout you won't feel the need to smoke for a few hours. Cravings might appear later on, but they surely are very week and soon enough it will be time for you to go to sleep. I personally divided my day in such a way, that while I am at work, distracted from smoking by my tasks, I wouldn't smoke. When I would get home I would rest for a bit and then go to the gym. Later on days passed without the puff with the support that came from my loved ones. For a person that just quit smoking, evenings are the hardest to resist cravings, but if you adopt physical exercise to your lifestyle, they can pass even without any withdrawal symptoms.

If you don't like the idea of going to the gym, I encourage you to do any kind of physical exercise like: swimming, dancing, cycling, yoga etc. Many smokers don't do any exercise because they either already have an appealing physical body or they simply feel fit, content with how they look. They consider it is a waste of time, they might not be fat, they don't need to lose the weight. But as I said, the point to do physical exercise here is not to lose weight, but to detoxify your body while keeping yourself busy and distracted from smoking. Cleansing your body this way will surely either reduce withdrawal symptoms or eliminate them in the first place. Through exercise you will also become stronger mentally and physically, simultaneously strengthening your lungs that have been charred by smoking.

To better understand why physical exercise is so important, we have to understand how it affects our brain. The first question we have to ask ourselves in this case is: why do we actually have a brain? Some would say that we need it to think, to come up with ideas, creative solutions to our day to day problems. The koala bear has adapted, over time, it's digestive system so that it can create the energy necessary for it to survive and function properly only through eucalyptus leaves. Because its main source of energy lies in a single tree, it doesn't move around very much. At the beginning of its evolutionary stage, the koala had a bigger brain, but over time is has narrowed its diet down and it needed less movement to find food sources and to survive. Less movement mint less cerebral function, thus resulting in a decrease of its brain size. The koala bear stays in a single tree for a long period of time. It can eat and even sleep there so it isn't exposed to threats from the ground. A big brain is necessary to facilitate complex movements. Executing these movements, together with a high cardiac rhythm, stimulates the brain into expanding. Physical exercise helps you learn easier, it helps you overcome stress and anxiety. It boosts focus. If, while engaging in physical exercise, you train your mind into discovering new things through listening to audio books or aching educative video clips, you facilitate your intellectual progress.

If you engage in physical exercise before learning, your study speed increases. The key to this phenomena is a brain derived neurotropic factors (BDNF). To be able to learn, the brain needs to grow and to modify its cellular structure to allow the neurons to function easier. BDNF improves this function, encourages this growth, strengthens it and protects it against the natural cell death in the brain. BDNF are a biological link between thought, emotions and movement. So, instead of drinking coffee, you could do a bit of physical exercise before learning.

An easier way to understand why physical exercise determines your brain to induce optimal study conditions is to imagine that your mind, your neuronal system, functions like an informatics system with the functions *if* and *then*. If it is cold, shake. If it is warm, sweat. Your body has triggers for any physiological process. This means that, regardless of the way you receive external stimuli

– olfactory, visually, acoustically, tactile – your brain has a series of responses ready to react. For instance, if gazelles hear movement in the grass, their brain reacts and processes a possible danger (summing up all possible factors like i.e.: the memory of past events, in which such movement in the grass may have led to attacks) by offering them a dose of adrenaline (to sharpen their senses and speed) and cortisol. Your brain works the same way: if you lay down on your bed all day you won't encourage it to progress. You become like the koala bear. You determine your brain to believe that everything is fine, that you can survive by continuing this lifestyle, without adding stress, without the need for progress. This happens when trying to quit ease well. You will never succeed in quitting if you don't offer the brain the necessary energy and motivation to conceive reasons on its own, not to stimulate you into continuing smoking, but to create reasons for you to become more healthy, more agile and independent. Similarly, it is as if you would spend a lot of money on a high-tech laptop while all you want to do is verify your emails with it. It doesn't make any sense, and your body, your mind, will notice this and will act accordingly. Without physical exercise you wouldn't progress in life and lecture. Lack of movement facilitates procrastination.

Thus, to lead a better life, we need to be always aware of our actions, of all the circumstances and deeds that influence us. This way will we be able to find a solution to improve our life and reach our desired result.

Activity signals the brain that something important is happening. Initially, it could signal the brain where food is to be found and how it can find it again. It can teach the brain how to escape an animal attack and how to avoid such an attack in the future. It works similarly now. The more you train yourself to quit smoking, the more you persist and keep fighting, the more you use positive thoughts regarding a non-smokers life, the faster you will learn these things and in short time they will be integrated into your neuronal network. Thus, the more you train yourself to quit smoking and explain yourself why it is beneficial for you to quit, the easier the actual process of quitting will be and you will start your life as a non-smoker without even experiencing withdrawal.

After engaging in physical activity, your body releases dopamine to motivate you to do more in the future. As it is a beneficial activity for your organism, it has to justify in a way the sweat and sacrifice – what better way to do it than dopamine? Leaving dopamine aside, physical exercise also increases your serotonin and noradrenalin levels. When the concentration levels in your body of these three neurotransmitters decrease, you tend to get depressed. If you feel like life has no meaning without a cigarette, do a bit of exercise for you to feel better. Don't smoke, you get further in your life through "running" towards your goals.

YOUR SMOKERS ENTOURAGE

You should avoid any smokers during at least your first few days as a non-smokers. I am not saying that you should cut the bonds you have with your friends or co-workers, neither am I saying you should become antisocial, but try distancing yourself from smokers in a constructive way. Think about friends who smoke and avoid them for at least a week until you settle down in your new life as a non-smoker or until you are sure you won't get tempted by anyone smoking around you. If you can't do so, at least ask them to abstain from smoking around you and to help you reach your goal easier. Find something else to do while others are smoking around you, or plan a holiday ahead. If you can't handle other people smoking around you, simply stay at home for a few days and explain to them what you are doing. I am sure they will respect your decision and even understand what you are going through.

If you really can't avoid any smokers, as I said, ask them not to offer you any cigarettes even if you get desperate. If you can't ask them such, walk away from them until they finished smoking. They won't smoke forever, so walking away for a few minutes shouldn't be an issue. You can continue any discussion you were in later on. If you stay while they're smoking, notice how the smell they give off is unpleasant, or wrap your head around the idea that they are currently burning their lungs. Ponder upon the fact that they don't really smoke because they are happy and can afford to do so, rather they are shackled by nicotine addiction which urges them toward this "suicidal" behaviour. You are free, you might even start to pity them and be grateful that you managed to fight this addiction. After they are done smoking, notice their smell on their cloths and breath. It's unpleasant, isn't it? Aren't you glad that nobody thinks such of you anymore? Observing smokers this way is now a perfect opportunity for you to realise what you left behind and how much you are prone to gain if you continue abstaining.

Don't let yourself get fooled if many of your friends smoke. This doesn't mean that they are better than you, cooler, more happy or energy. They don't actually want to smoke, but they do so by the nicotine's bidding. They have a voice that enslaves them and they will start justifying their behaviour, and even lie to you that what they do brings them joy and happiness. But you already know that this is just a nicotine created lie, an illusion. Don't let yourself be tempted and fooled, resist until you are indeed free.

Smokers will try to fool you, especially the ones that claim that they smoke either few cigarettes per day, or the ones that claim to smoke only when they want to, not that they have to do so to quell their "thirst". They will claim that they can smoke whenever they like and they smoke only out of pure pleasure. You know very well by now that this is impossible. If they don't smoke at 10 am. , but smoke at 11 or 12 doesn't mean that they decided to smoke when they wanted. It might be the case nicotine cravings kicked in at a later hour, rather than earlier, or that they simply did not have the occasion before. Maybe a meal, alcohol or something else triggered them, but fact is, their body asked them to smoke. They simply don't claim any responsibility and don't admit their addiction, but fact is that justification for such a compulsive behaviour is born out of ignorance towards reality. Occasional smokers puff more often then they admit anyway. Don't let yourself be fooled by the thought that you could do so to, drastically reduce the numbers of cigarettes per day and only have a few. Each puff contains nicotine, thus leading to further addiction. Each puff is lethal on the long run. Anyways, if you do decide to drastically reduce the cigarettes you smoke per day and somehow manage to respect this limit, after a while you will surely forget about this goal and sooner or later you will get back to smoking as much as before. Once you start quitting, you are in this for good. Smoking less is only a justification, a way developed by the subconscious mind to keep you smoking.

Let's get back to the justifications of smokers. People like to be right. It bothers us to be told we are wrong. We like to be free and we certainly don't like to feel constrained. People seek out justifications to the acts they are doing and don't really care if they are wrong, as long as other people agree with them. That's why smokers smoke more when they are next to other smokers, rather than non-smokers that might judge them. Synthesising, we realise that we feel much better, as smokers, around other smokers. We seek to validate the vice because deep down we know it hurts us, but since others do it as well, it seems alright. We might think it's perfectly justifiable. Anything can be told to us, as long as we are sustained by a smokers "community", we simply won't even consider quitting, never so much as changing our mind and beliefs about smoking. In the moment in which you quit for good and while you adopt and consolidate this new lifestyle, smokers will start justifying themselves towards you. They might even try to convince you to continue smoking, otherwise, they will feel guilty for not quitting themselves. They prefer pulling you down rather than admitting that they too could lead a better life. Don't let yourself be influenced by them. This is precisely why I have recommend you earlier to avoid such situations, until you are stronger and can resist any temptation. Try at least understanding what happens in their mind, why they are trying to convince you to continue and why they are trying to take down your quitting plan. If they don't try, they admit their own failure. They don't do it out of wickedness, but out of a self-defence instancing that is propelled by their nicotine addiction.

NON-SMOKER ENTOURAGE

Try imagining how those around you look at you, especially the non-smokers. How do you smell to them? Do you like walking on the street while a car passes by that exhausts lots of smoking making you unable to breathe for a few moments? You cough and swear a lot. Well, this is how non-smokers feel around you. You are like a car's exhaustion pipe. When you don't smoke, you reek anyway. People only stand beside you because you probably mean something to them, or they can't get away from you, co-workers for example. Nevertheless, a stranger will avoid you for the mere fact that you smell.

You might seem weak in the eyes of a non-smoker. They can handle life very well without smoking and they can't imagine why you are smoking, why you can't simply quit. You can't control yourself and you succumb to such a meaningless addiction. You seem like a week person, undoable to abstain from a vice. Then I ask you, what you are capable of, if you can't even take care of yourself and your own health? Look at the non-smokers around you. How are they spending their time? Would cigarettes improve their lifestyle as you think they are improving yours? Did you ever notice that they don't need cigarettes to be happy, to enjoy meals, breaks, events, to have fun or to simply live life to the fullest? To write, focus, think, communicate or be active? You don't need them either, you will soon see.

Try spending as much time as possible around non-smokers, maybe even try to seek out some friends that have quit smoking and talk to them about how you are planning to quit yourself. They might come up with good ideas to help you get rid of this harmful addiction or they might even support you, check up and you and encourage you to continue. Do this especially if you experience cravings, ask them for advice and support. They are able to demonstrate to you, psychologically and physically, that it is possible to quit. They have managed to overcome this vice, thereby you are able to do so too.

It is very important for you to pay attention to non-smokers. See what they are doing, how they are filling their time and learn from it. We tend to create the illusion that they are bored and don't savour life as well as smokers. I admit that I myself have had the same feeling. I considered them boring, or rather bored and unable to enjoy a sunset like we do while smoking. I was wrong. Without cigarettes, the colours of a sunset seem more alive, and now I can clearly see how wrong I was before. While smoking, you don't really focus on the activity you are doing, the music you listen to or the sunset you are watching, rather you are according most of your focus to the act of smoking, enabling you to fully experiencing whatever you are doing. Truth be told, when you pay more attention to non-smokers, you find that they are even more relaxed than smokers are. They don't have the extra stress provided by cigarettes (i.e.: do I still have cigarettes or money to buy a new pack?) and they don't seek situation in which they can escape whatever event they are participating at to be able to smoke, they don't go and stand outside in the rain or cold to smoke. Non-smokers have more willpower and are able to fulfill their goals easier through it. Smokers often loath themselves, they feel less motivated and their self-esteem is low. Thus, they may come to imagine that they will never succeed in life, as they have never succeeded into quitting smoking.

Once you quit, you will see how many wonderful achievements you can accomplish in life, because you change your mentality and you will discover that you are way stronger than the addiction. You will confront stress and hard situation with ease. You will have the power to do so. If you are capable of quitting smoking, you are capable of doing anything you wish in life.

The only advantage you currently have opposed to a non-smoker that has never smoked is the fact that now, with this burning flame and ambition inside yourself, you will be able to quit smoking while personally developing yourself and straightening your life. You wake up to reality and understand not only that smoking destroys you, but that quitting will transform your existence to a much better one. While a non-smoker might have no reason or battle to take, you will fight for a new life and through the inertia continue to do so in other aspects as well.

THE DIFFERENCE BETWEEN AN EX-SMOKER AND A NON-SMOKER

After you quit, don 'say that you quit smoking, rather present yourself simply as a non-smoker. When smokers declare that they quit smoking, you can feel some sense of sacrifice in their words. It sounds like they have lost some part of their identity. This can put the process of quitting in a bad, negative, light, making it harder. You might end up obsessed with the idea of renouncing something important, that relaxes you. But, once you start your journey as a non-smoker, you will look at smoking in another light. You will then see that smoking does not bring you any benefit, so you don't sacrifice actually anything.

I know this might not seem very important to you, but believe me that it helps a lot, especially by integrating in your mind the idea that it isn't hard to quit smoking, that you aren't making an actually sacrifice, or that you didn't make one. Another difference is, that if you see yourself as an ex-smoker, instead of a non-smoker, you let the impression that smoking was once part of your personality, you identity, a part of your life. You shouldn't let the past define your present. The past has contributed to the formation of your personality but now you are a different person, prone to continuous change. Those who consider themselves ex-smokers still long for a smoke. They didn't completely get over this addiction, on a psychological level at least, and nostalgia might cover them each time this subject is mentioned. They feel sorry that they stopped smoking and they feel as a part of their personality has been ripped off, probably by someone else's impulse.

If you are still smoking, repeat in your mind, with joy, enthusiasm and eagerness: "I'm gonna be a non-smoker and I am happy I am taking this step in my life." When you are a non-smoker, repeat: "I have made the right choice in becoming a non-smoker. My life is turning to the better. I am very happy with my current situation." Repeat these phrases as often as possible, even now. Write them down and put them in various place so you may remember them more often. If you experience any cravings repeat them and add your own word: "I must resist this craving a bit longer, it will soon pass. I am strong and I can resist it. After that, glorious things await." Repeat these phrases out loud, but not while smoking, because your mind could make bad associations between these phrases and the fact that you are turning into a non-smoker.

THE LITTLE THINGS

Once you turn into a non-smoker, you will have so much time and energy at your disposable that you won't know what to do with them. At that moment, your lifestyle will improve. Enjoy the little things in life. Besides the fact that they are good, alternative, dopamine sources, they will teach you how to live life to its fullest. If you are still smoking, it is definitely hard for you to imagine how such a new life could be, but I am telling you now that you have to prepare for it. The food will taste better, it will be more sonorous. It will smell better. You will be able to smell the fresh scent of bloomed flowers in the spring. You will enjoy swimming more and feel more intensely how the water slips on your skin. When we are smokers, nothing else concerns us but the next moment, opportunity, to smoke. Instead of enjoying our surroundings, we seek such occasions to slip away and light one up. Maybe you consider that cigarettes gave you time to reflect upon your problems. To be able to smoke, you have to stop doing whatever you do, take a small break and so you consider you are making time to ponder upon your life. You will see once you are a non-smoker that you were wrong. You will have more time to observe the details of matters, instead of letting your mind be clouded by nicotine cravings. While being a smoker, while you were beside loved ones, were you truly present? Analyze this well. You might want to look at non-smokers, how they act, how they interact, how they breathe, how they live. Interact with them. You will have much more time at your disposal once your mind stops nagging you to smoke and once you don't spend your time smoking, but with people. Strengthen your bonds with them by offering your presence.

When you go out into society, analyze strangers. Pay more attention to them. In the past, the cigarette might have distracted you. You were smoking, so your mind and subconscious were always busy. You could stand beside someone without even talking, being busy smoking. Imagine how funny it would be if two people stood next to each other and had nothing else to do but look at each other or at the ground. Cigarettes are a way to distract us and to exempt us from conversations. Now you can tie stronger bonds with other peoples or establish new ones. Get involved into conversations more actively. Be present. Notice your surroundings and talk about them. If you are next to a smoker, study him. Try imagining why he is smoking. What is your opinion about him? Does he really enjoy the cigarette or does he repress his cravings while intoxicating himself? Does he really feel well inhaling all those noxious toxins instead of enjoying life? Is he really glad to smoke or is he simply pleasing his inner demons that constantly urge him to smoke? You are stronger. You don't need cigarettes. You can easily tell that they are the week ones, not you for desiring change and freedom.

Start creating order in your life. Literally and figuratively. You have more time and energy at your disposal as a non-smoker, so use it to live tidier—every time you are bored make sure to clean your drawer and wardrobe, your room, your office, but also start reading, socialize. Keep your mind busy and work on your physique. Use time at your disposal for progressive behaviour. Not only will you forget about cravings and withdrawal, but gradually you will create a brilliant, beautiful, tidy, and orderly life for yourself. Such small achievements add up and happen to be the building blocks of a successful life.

At the beginning, you will need to keep your time busy actively and consciously. After a while everything will come naturally. Start enjoying the small victories that are added to your life day by day, and soon enough you will crave for more achievements. Don't let yourself be discouraged if what I say seems exhausting to you. With the extra dose of energy you will receive once your body is rid of the toxins that are slowing it down, you will be able to accomplish more than you can now, as a smoker, imagine. Things will flow naturally, your life will be more orderly, fulfilled and active, and your subconscious, instead of asking you to smoke, will start asking you to do more such beneficial actions for yourself. If you start feeling that you have wasted time and money through smoking in the past, you will find that you are slowly recovering all that has been lost. The process of becoming a non-smoker is demanding and requires lots of physical and mental effort. But these are so-called bonuses, compared to someone who has never smoked before, because they were never required to go through such hardships, so they will not get the impulse for change in life, and inertia won't lead them where it will lead you once you start reclaiming your life from nicotine.

A way I used to "kill time" when I became a non-smoker was to pay more attention to my surroundings and my life. I tried, and it seemed easier to me than before, to analyse why certain events happen in my life and so I managed to find solutions to certain problems much easier. I admit, sometimes I did experience tobacco cravings, but they didn't last long and once they have passed, I would continue embracing life. I noticed I can improve my life and those around me. Instead of wasting time smoking, I was paying more attention to small details in life that previously might have passed unnoticed. Maybe I simply replaced an "illness" with another, but hear me out: I paid more attention to the needs of my loved ones. I saw things that I previously could not, because at the time I was distracting myself either with smoking or the thought of smoking. This fogged my mind so I couldn't really focus on other people. Now I am able to see the slightest details, the essence of things, the subtle needs of my loved ones and I can notice that through me I can improve the life's of others. I started enjoying the little things and started creating such little joys in the life of others.

Each time you are tempted to smoke, inhale deeply and smile while thinking how much joy you are bringing to others and how much your presence means to them. Don't leave your family or loved ones to go out smoking, try to enjoy their company. Don't choose smoking over time with your family, don't kill yourself slowly with tobacco, rather allow yourself to live more and offer them a lifetime of joy through your existence. Smile while thinking of your accomplishment and be proud of yourself. You made an extremely important step in life and you will continue to thread on this new path, destined only for the strong.

POSTPONEMENT

Since you made it this far, in case you are considering to wait a bit longer until you quit, I am advising you not to postpone. This will only encourage your into thinking that you don't really desire to quit and it will make it even harder for yourself to do so, even if you re-read the book in the future.

Maybe you will pick a day in the near future when you decide to quit, but when the day comes, you decide it really isn't the right time actually. A sudden event might appear, a new dilemma in your life, a fight with your loved ones. Or maybe yet you do start the process of becoming a non-smoker, and after a day you realise how unhappy you are – you are lacking focus, everything seems miserable in your life, you don't need the extra stress from cravings. Once again, you might postpone quitting. Since you have read the book until this point, you should understand that the right moment will never come as long as you allow your brain to constantly fool you into contusing to smoke with various reasons as such. Life has ups and downs. You will never find the right moment to quit. Don't postpone anymore and assume responsibility for your initial decision to become a non-smoker. Pick your date in which you quit, right now.

Focus on what really matters. Develop the ability to distinguish what is important in life and what is meaningless. Often we dedicate our time and energy to small tasks – in example, you move and object from one place to another and you consider tidying your place up this way – that don't really influence our lives, but, as they are easy to complete, they offer us the sensation that we have accomplished something big. The mind perceives the need for change and organizing, but you consciously focus on meaningless tasks and you seek to postpone or push aside the meaningful ones, the ones that could actually impact your life. You seek to solve such small problems, while ignoring the big one in fear of real, meaningful, change. You may receive dopamine on the spot for solving such minor tasks, but the quality of your life does not improve. The same happens when you postpone quitting too. Is there any reason for you to really postpone quitting now? Are you postponing out of serious reasons or only because you are afraid to fee reality?

Your mind will start conceiving a lot of reasons for you to continue smoking and postponing the day you become a non-smoker. In a few weeks you have to attend a wedding or an event, better quit after that, right? Soon enough New Year's Eve will come, you will quit after that night so you can have fun at that event. You don't need to fight withdrawal and cravings on Christmas and New Year's Eve. You have more things in plan than you usually do, better let this busy period in your life pass so you can focus on quitting afterwards. A perfect timing to quit will never appear. The more you postpone, the farther away the day in which you quit will be, and it might eventually never come. You don't want to do it because holidays appear, because you have lots of work to do... then when?

Should you choose a day to quit in the distant future, you could forget about it and your enthusiasm to quit will die until that date arrives. Emotionally and physically you live under the impression that you may have more time to prepare until then, but the truth is that your mind will create new "pleasant" memories regarding smoking by that time and it will be harder for you to quit.

It may happen that you pick a day in the near future, but when the moment comes you don't feel ready, prepared to embrace this new lifestyle. If you quit at the pre-set date, you find that you are unhappy, you need more focus to finish your tasks (that never end) or everything is so miserable in your life that you simply can't handle this change. You don't want to worsen your situation with cravings and withdrawal, so you postpone again. By now you should really understand that the right moment to quit will never appear as long as you allow your brain to constantly fool you with various excuses and reasons to smoke. You will never find a right moment, an optimal period of time. Please, don't postpone anymore and set the date in which you will quit. The process takes **seven** days.

In these seven days, together we will prepare to quit smoking. I started working on this book while I was still smoking. Ok, not actually while I was smoking. I was looking for possibilities to quit. I never succeeded. Each time I tried, I failed. This is because I never had something to rely on, a plan or even information about what measures I should take to quit. At a certain point, I started writing down ideas, notes, I started informing myself about what it actually means to smoke, how it affects the body, what effects nicotine has upon it, how we are psychologically linked to smoking and so on. I wrote down the main ideas and I managed to conceive a "battle plan". I learned what my biggest enemy was(nicotine), and how to fight it. So far, you have followed a few preparations yourself: you learn what smoking on a biological level means, then on a psychological level, and you acquired a few information regarding the preparations you have to take for this "war" on nicotine. Now, the conception of a more elaborate plan begins, writing the "battle plan" down, and soon enough, the so-said assault.

Through the above mentioned, written down,

notes, ideas and through my personal journal in which I monitored my vices, withdrawal symptoms and the measures taken, this chapter has been created. For 7 days I have prepared myself to quit in every way possible so I can embrace with ambition and power the day in which I become a non-smoker. These days will help you prepare physically and mentally and pre-adapt you to a non-smokers life. Due to them, you will greet your first day as a non-smoker, especially because you know exactly when that day is, and you will have time to leave any thoughts of smoking aside. If I would ask you to quit smoking right now, you would get scared, discouraged and find several reasons to continue, at least for a few more days. Now, you have 7 days at your disposal to accept the fact that you are going to quit. It is time to anticipate the stress inducing situations in your life that will trigger you to smoke, and you will have to find ways to either avoid them, or confront them.

I recommend you finish reading this book so you can get a general picture of everything. Then come back to this chapter and start your "battle-plan". "Save a date", seven days from now, in which you become a non-smoker for life.

Don't expect moments of revelation that should determine you to quit. You will wait in vain. Nothing works like this, only if it is maybe too late. The revelation you are tempted to wait for is, actually, another excuse conceived by your mind to postpone the moment in which you quit. Our mind is uneducated regarding smoking and that is why we continue to do so. Before reading this book, you were never really educated regarding the subject of smoking. Gradually, with each page, you understood what this destructive act means. The earlier mentioned, long awaited, revelation has been gradually created, through learning slowly, and that is why you don't experience a thrilling feeling through your body and mind. The subconscious started to readjust itself and to support you on your way into becoming a non-smoker. If you would have received all the information in this book suddenly, you would have been overwhelmed by dopamine and you would have felt such a miraculous, thrilling feeling in your body. But this isn't physically possible, so don't wait for miracles any longer. If it would have been this easy, a miracle-solution to quit smoking would have been long found and advertised thoroughly. If you passively wait your entire life for something to happen to you, well, your life will pass by, without you participating in it or taking any action and responsibility to better it.

You have to want to accept change. You create everything that surrounds you, your own reality, as you have created the reality of a smoker's life. Now that you know all the information in this book, I am firmly convinced that you desire such change, at least more than you did before. If you still have doubts, read the book to the end, and if you then feel the same, simply follow blindly what I have written in this book, without thinking too much, and try respecting each step in my "battle plan". Take care; these doubts might be fueled by your subconscious which would still like you to cling to your smoker's life. As I said, the subconscious does not like change, whether it is god or bad. You will succeed; you just have to believe you can. Re-read this book as many times as necessary. Take notes, underline ideas that you consider work best for you and read them as often as possible.

It is said that if you don't know where you are heading, you don't know when you are going to get there. It is challenging to make drastic changes in your life, but, if you set realistic goals, it is less stressful.

THE DAY IN WHICH YOU BECOME A NON-SMOKER

It is good to organize. Not only now, but in general. Maybe you haven't noticed yet, but the best results in life are due to a well set plan. You thus know what you have to do, from beginning to the end, how to do it. Starting such a well-planned task is easy, carrying them out is with great ease and joy since you know exactly how to handle the issues you may face along. By ending them, a great sense of satisfaction and victory awaits. If you "fight" on accomplishing tasks without even knowing where to start, not to mention not knowing where they lead, you will surely, naturally, fail. It is better to systemize the approach and the work-process of a problem. You develop a plan of action. That is how we will proceed now.

It is important to choose the exact date in which you will become a non-smoker. If you do it suddenly, without any preparation, from one day to another, you have big chances of relapsing. Hereby, if you choose the exact day, you have a week time to prepare yourself emotionally, psychologically and physically. You will cleanse your body of toxins so you may have lesser withdrawal symptoms, you will educate your mind, so it may not ever fool you into smoking again, but making it support your fight against nicotine.

I recommend you start on Friday, so smoke your last cigarette on Thursday. You will still have nicotine reserves in your body on Friday from the previous day, thus on Friday you can go to work and abstain easily from smoking. The body won't yet notice the decrease in nicotine and the subconscious won't notice what you are planning to do. That is why, on the first day, you won't experience hard cases of nicotine withdrawal. When you get home from work, rest for a while and go to the gym to remove the toxins from your body, to oxygenize your blood, to vitalize yourself and to keep your mind and spare time busy. After you engage in physical exercise, you don't feel the need to smoke anymore for a few hours. Once you arrive home, it will be too late for you to experience any more cravings. Spend the weekend at home, with your family if possible, ask them you help and keep an eye on you as you might be tempted to buy cigarettes.

It doesn't really matter what day of the week it is. You will begin the process of becoming a non-smoker regardless and we will make it unfold smoothly. Now, preparations follow. We will use the resources from the previous chapters; I will repeat some of them without getting into further details anymore. By now you should know and understand them anyway.

Use the next, preparatory, seven days more as a guide meant to give you some suggestions. You already know your goal, where they are heading, now I will tell you how to walk this road. Maybe you don't manage to follow everything exactly, but try hard and add your own ideas to these seven days. I guarantee it will be extremely easy to become a non-smoker. Read all the indications and apply them all in one day, or at least one each day, but act upon them constantly.

DAY -7

This is the most demanding day from all the ones that will follow. You have a lot to work on it and it would be best if you would do the tasks progressively so you may not feel overwhelmed. The required tasks don't really take up much time, but they do require maximum attention. Try solving most of your small issues, tasks so you won't have to handle them next week as a non-smoker. In example, if you kept postponing an unpleasant phone call, do it now. If you need to meet a person that you kept avoiding, meet them now. Don't leave room for surprises and irritating tasks you might have to face next week. Anticipate and try solving anything that may arise, right now.

Most people consider that it is best to quit smoking suddenly, instead of reducing your cigarette servings. This is because, usually, reducing the number of cigarettes smoked per day can make us forget about our goals and at a certain point we end up smoking as much as we did before. However, you have an exact date in mind and this will not allow you to fall into this trap.

You are allowed to smoke in these seven days, but not much. I suggest you smoke the minimum required to you physically, so you may focus on the tasks you have to do to prepare yourself for the big day. I smoked about two packs a day, that's about 40 cigarettes. If you smoke this same amount, it will probably be hard to reduce the number to 3-4 per day, but try. From those 40 per day, you most likely need only about four or five, so you can diminish any cravings that might make you "mad". You simply smoke the others as fillers, out of boredom or simply because habitually you don't even notice lighting them up. Reduce the number of cigarettes smoked per day right now; it will make things easier for you on the first days as a non-smoker.

Try feeling each cigarette. I mean smoke "consciously", notice how you inhale the smoke, how it chars your lungs, how it dries your mouth up, how it deprives you from oxygen, how you start smelling badly and how your brain starts fogging up. Realize what you are doing and how harmful it is to you. Don't think about anything else while smoking these few cigarettes, only about the act itself and what happens to you. Ask yourself, why are you smoking those cigarettes in the first place? Did you really have to? Do you even have to finish the cigarette up, or are just some puffs enough? Analyse the taste of the cigarette. Is it really as pleasant as you think it is or can you feel the chemicals though? Think about how you are burning your money away with each puff, how you could have spent your time with your loved ones instead of smoking. How will you smell to them afterwards? It's hard to consciously engage in such a noxious behaviour, but you have to proceed this way during these days, especially if you didn't yet convince your subconscious about the harms done by a cigarette. These are perfect exercises to do so. Don't think about how a cigarette calms you down anymore, you can realize it isn't so. Ask yourself, each time you smoke, if they really bring you joy or if they simply remove the discomfort that the lack of nicotine provides. The answer is the latter, and you just don't want to allow this further.

During these days I personally started smoking cigarettes with less nicotine, tar and carbon monoxide. I am not saying that those cigarettes are better, but I started getting my body used to less nicotine and I filled my lungs with less tar, which allowed me to engage in physical activity and to breathe easier, thus increasing my mental acuity. Now, your purpose isn't to simply reduce the number of cigarettes, but to slowly "untrain" yourself from smoking and to demonstrate to yourself that you can control this habit. You discipline yourself into smoking less; you thereby strengthen your willpower. When you start your life as a non-smoker, you will realise that since you had the power to smoke less than before, you will realize that you can even not smoke at all and that you have the willpower to resist temptation. It will also be physically easier for you. Your body will ask for less nicotine and the dopamine receptors will start healing themselves gradually.

Watch out not to fool yourself and wallow through a false sense of progress. If you did manage to reduce the number of cigarettes that you smoke per day, or if you are smoking less nicotine containing cigarettes, doesn't mean that you are rid of smoking for good. If you smoked inside your car while driving, stop doing that. If you smoke while enjoying your coffee, stop. Make smoking uncomfortable while trying to lit cigarettes up only in unusual and unpleasant places, for example, in front of your house. Or you could simply try not smoking at all while at home or at your work. It would be much better such way since you would disassociate these pleases with smoking. Smoke those three to four cigarettes until you arrive home and you can spend the rest of your day enjoying your time with your loved ones. They will surely distract you from smoking.

In the preparatory seven days, I have seeked small but efficient tasks to do. They were meant to improve my lifestyle in general while distracting me, through activity, from smoking. I hoped to integrate them to my lifestyle while practicing them daily. And I succeeded. I have spent each day more time on improving my appearance, through exercise, grooming, but also through turning my diet into a healthier one. Before I would leave the house I would shave, even if it was not really necessary. I would clean my shoes up, even though they weren't really dirty.

Performing all these new tasks will give you the feeling that you are busier than before. Maybe you can't find room to fit all of these into your daily routine. But if you think about it, you usually wasted about 4 minutes on each cigarette – so surely it isn't a big deal to allocate a few minutes to tidy your life up. Give yourself more attention, this way you will also signal the subconscious the need and will to change to the better, not only in the context of health but also physical aspect.

Calculate how much money you have wasted since you started smoking up until now. Calculate how much money you spend on smoking each month. Write these sums down so you can analyse them each time you might be tempted to smoke. Don't worry. You might have wasted lots of money on smoking, but it isn't the world's end. Don't let anxiety grasp you when you see the total sum, but let yourself be embraced by the possibility of recovering all this lost money and time. Maybe it would seem impossible, but I will explain to you, in short, how you will recover them. You will have more energy to fulfil your tasks without being interrupted by smoking. Your intellectual capacity will increase, thus allowing you a higher focus on whatever you are doing, while raising your efficiency to perform those tasks. You will be a lot more active than before, more attentive and involved in your tasks. There are non-smokers that suffer from procrastination. You won't allow yourself to push anything aside anymore, knowing how much you have already lost. Firstly, the new wave of energy you will experience will give you an incentive and you will start rectifying your life in ways in which you may have never imagined. Secondly, you will occupy your mind with various activities to distract yourself from smoking, activities which without doubt will boost your enthusiasm for progress. Even if you may have lost a lot of time due to smoking so far, you will start a new life of a non-smoker with a stronger psyche and physique, ready to confront any difficulties.

I won't ask you to do any more lists, but if you have the necessary ambition, then create one with the tasks that need to be done in these seven preparatory days, extra to the ones mentioned earlier: read 10 pages of a book per day, do at least 10 minutes of physical exercise or any other things that can keep you busy and bring progress to your life. Drink more water, especially if you feel the need to smoke. Sometimes, thirst can be mistaken with cigarette cravings.

DAY -6

Stop smoking in places where you are used to do so, and stop doing associations between cigarettes and other things, like drinking coffee...Break these patterns and associations. If you are used to smoking at home, stop smoking there. If you are used to smoking while driving, stop doing that.

As a fresh non-smoker, the smell of cigarettes will only torment you and bring you memories of the past days, in which you have smoked. So clean up your car if you used to smoke inside. Wash it, remove any smells that might reside through fresheners and stop smoking inside it for the following days. If your clothes smell of smoke, wash them and add some perfume to your closet so they smell nice all the time. Stop smoking inside your house, go outside regardless if it is raining, snowing or extremely hot. If you live in a flat, stop smoking on the balcony, rather go downstairs to have a cigarette, or any other place that might make it hard for you to smoke. Your target should be to make smoking as difficult as possible in this time period, and also distancing yourself from the usual smoking places.

Throw out all your ashtrays, from your household or from your workplace, if you haven't already done this. This will create a discomfort for the few cigarettes that you are still allowed to smoke. You won't need them in a few days anyway and if you receive guests that smoke, simply tell them that you don't allow smoking at your place. It's your turn to be the annoying host without ashtrays. Freshen your house with calming sprays like jasmine or lavender. If the smell of smoke is still intense, try buying some anti-tobacco sprays. You will find that they mask the smell of smoke surprisingly well.

Start doing exercise beginning today. Don't postpone any longer, the more you do, the less are the chances of you ever starting. Furthermore, if you start exercising now, you will get used to physical exercise and you will be able to integrate this into your routine, so when you are a non-smoker you won't have to use your willpower on getting started. If you have had a hard day so far, start with light physical exercise. Breathe in deeply before starting. Do some crunches, pushups, stretches, actually any kind of physical exercise you can engage into at home or at your workplace. If you feel tired, think again, are you really unable to do some exercise? I am sure you will find the energy for a few sets. Exercise will also invigorate you and start your metabolism, so if you do a few exercises you will surely obtain some extra energy for the rest of the day.

If you have enough time, go to the gym and make a subscription, or at least try jogging outdoors. You will have to do exercise as often as possible so you can ward off any future withdrawal symptoms, so it would be best to warm up now.

You don't have to renounce all your vices at once. But during this transition it would be ideal if you could avoid some triggers that could make you want to smoke, for instance: morning coffee. Maybe this previous sentence would make you want to stop reading right now... but please don't, for your own sake, hear me out. Try at least not to smoke at all while drinking your coffee. I know it feels good, but you will further support this trigger and once you are a non-smoker, drinking coffee could remind you of smoking, thus inducing some cravings. It would be best if you would start breaking this link between these two. If you need the extra energy provided by coffee, try drinking it as fast as possible and then wash your mouth so you can get rid of the smoking-triggering taste. However, you would recommend you should use black tea instead or any other natural energizers. It will be a lot easier to break the link this way and you would still receive the required amount of energy you need to tackle your day. Try not lighting a cigarette up right after you finish drinking your coffee. Wait at least an hour so your subconscious won't tie the two actions together anymore. I don't think I should mention this, but I will anyway: try not lighting a cigarette up even before drinking coffee, even if it isn't at the same time. Allow some space between these actions.

Utter positive affirmations like: "I am eager to begin my new life as a non-smoker", "I embrace the change that will come because I know for sure it

will make my life much better", "I have long
awaited the day in which I become a non-smoker,
finally it is time to achieve this goal". Repeat all
these sentences as often as possible, even aloud, or
at least in your own mind, but repeat then. Your
subconscious might start "reacting" to these
affirmations and try to pull you down, so you
continue smoking, but you have to clarify to it that
nothing bad will happen and that you truly wish
change. You find it ridiculous doing such
affirmations? No problem, look up on the internet
motivations quotes suitable for your needs and
personality, save them and read them occasionally
out loud (when you are alone), until they embed
into your mind.

Day -5

Do you remember my ginger recipe? I didn't
joke about it, it is really beneficial. It helps your
metabolism, it cleanses your body and it invigorates
you. You will feel much better eating it and if you
do it consciously, you might even receive dopamine
as a reward for the fact that you are doing
something healthy for your body. If you don't like
the taste of ginger, you can start an alternative
detoxification method using tea. You should cleanse
your body up to the day you become a non-smoker
and you should get used to having a healthy body.
You can continue cleansing your body using such

detoxification methods even in your new life as a non-smoker. It will surely aid your body in its fight against withdrawal. Anyways, it is healthy to start such detox processes, they will invigorate you, clear your mind while removing any brain fog you might experience. The subconscious will assume this new information and will help you, even ask you to further engage in detoxifying your body and to readjust your lifestyle in general.

Take more walks with your loved one or meet up with non-smoking friends. Don't smoke while you are with them, even if you still have a threshold of those 3-4 daily allowed cigarettes. You should be trying to break the link of smoking while with others here, so you can see that you can enjoy yourself and have fun around other people even if you aren't smoking. Aim to smoke the remaining cigarettes before you go out, or after, if possible, at all. Seek to do various activities like going to the theatre, opera, the movies or any events that are disabling you to smoke. Through such events, seek personal growth and progress, culture yourself or simply relax. If you can, try joining a charity organization, a book-club or a workshop of any kind.

Try finding new hobbies. You still have a few days at your disposal to do so. Some say a great stress reliever is drawing or colouring. There is a great variety of adult colouring books available. You can keep them handy in moments while talking on the phone, or when you are bored. Actually, in any moment in which you could experience cravings. Colouring should keep you busy and relieve withdrawal-caused stress. Instead of lighting a cigarette up, doodle in such a book until you relax. If you don't have any ideas for a specific hobby, well I can't help you, you have to discover something you like on your own. Search for online events and creative workshops, give a few a try until you actually find something suitable for you. You can even look up online what other people use as hobbies, like: crafting, origami, painting, swimming and others.

If you are unable to discover any hobby, don't alarm yourself, there are alternatives, too. My passion resides in self-development. I actually use this as a hobby: I dedicate my free time reading through various blogs, self-development books or listening to online motivational speakers. It inspires me to do so, my time is kept busy, it helps me disconnect from the daily stress, while I learn new things through the experience of others that could aid me in life.

DAY -4

If you have managed to apply what I have suggested to you in the previous days, then you have made some significant progress in your life. Take some time to ponder upon these progresses, and how they are different to your past lifestyle. I am sure you can either see improvement in life or you can foresee some in the near future. You also demonstrate perseverance and that you are willing to become a non-smoker. Now it is time to tell as much people as possible about your intentions and what you wish to pursue, to realise. Tell your friends about your intentions of becoming a non-smoker, tell them the date you have fixed and ask them to help you in the upcoming period. Do you know someone who has quit in the past? Talk to them and ask them for their aid and advice. Ask them to check up on you daily, through phone calls or messages asking you about your progress. Watch out, ex-smokers tend to dramatize, we all like a bit of drama and victimization so we are better appreciated for our effort. Some will say it easy for them to quit, others will say it is hard. The latter people either did not have such a help as you do, through this book, or they exaggerate. They might have even quit because they had to, not because they wanted to, so they are still clinging to their past life and look upon quitting with regret. I can tell you honestly that it isn't hard at all, as long as you respect the psychological and physiological needs of your body.

Seeking out a mentor is essential because you would feel like disappointing them if you fail. Ask your loved one, a family member or a friend to be such a mentor and support you through your struggles. Tell them about your plan of action, about what you wish to accomplish and how, such that they can form a general idea about what is going to happen.

Start doing breathing exercises. Inhale deeply, slowly and then exhale all the air, slowly. These exercises will oxygenate your blood and brain; they will give you energy and maybe even motivation. Force yourself to do these exercises as often as possible until they get automated; they will help you whenever you experience any cravings. Do you remember the word replacement exercise, in which I asked you to replace the word "cigarettes" with "air" in the sentence: "I need a cigarette"? You can re-read the chapter again to freshen your memory up. If cravings test your patience, abstain from smoking by exercising this technique for the following days and in the days as a non-smoker.

DAY -3

It is time to take a healthier diet into consideration and to analyse what food you have in your kitchen. Start replacing your unhealthy food progressively with healthy ones so once your appetite recovers from quitting smoking you have them at hand: carrots, nuts and other nutritious and nourishing foods, without fats.

Trust me, you don't want to experience hunger pangs with a collection of junk food and sodas at home. You don't have to completely remove these from your diet (although I do recommend it). You can consume them further whenever you desire. The idea is that you don't make stocks of them at home and don't have them handy so you can eat at any time. Buy them occasionally and just as a small treat, not a huge bag. Instead of sodas, you can drink carbonated water. Personally, I was a huge fan of caffeine rich drinks like energizers, or various coffee products. I noticed I can quell my thirst for these if I simply drink carbonated water. Still water doesn't have any taste. Instead of sodas, you can drink water with just a right amount of syrup to appease your sweet tooth. This is how I proceed now. Water with a bit of syrup contains less sugar than any drink you could buy in a store. Don't forget, you can eat and drink anything when going out, we are currently only discussing the foods you eat and keep at home and at work, the places you spend most of your time at.

Take it slow, don't push yourself, you don't need to fight cravings for sweets as well during the upcoming period, but you do have to take care on what you eat and drink, due to the metabolic changes you are about to experience.

It is recommended that you wash your teeth two times a day. Try using mint flavoured toothpaste. Menthol represses the need to smoke and freshens your breath. You won't feel any need to smoke as long as that freshness persists in your mouth. Alternatively, chew sugar-less, mint-flavoured chewing-gum. Any times you start experiencing a craving, chew a gum. I bet you know what a horrible taste a cigarette has when smoking it with mint essence in your mouth. Disgusting really, so I bet you won't be tempted to smoke while you can still feel the mint flavour.

DAY -2

Great things await you. If you have not yet made a list with all the beneficial change in your new life as a non-smoker, it is time you create it now. Write everything you wish to achieve with the new energy you will gain and with all the savings you will make.

If you haven't done it yet, it's time to create a life plan. Try setting realistic goals so you won't get disappointed. For instance, everybody would like to be a millionaire, but few can succeed. I am not saying you shouldn't try to be one, but I recommend aiming towards being as happy as a millionaire. What does this mean? Imagine how one leads his life, and how you can live it similarly. What would you do if you'd had an endless amount of money? Well, try doing that, at least at a lower scale. If a millionaire would travel to tropical islands, I bet you can at least afford to go to a beach either near you, or at a cheaper place. Sand is sand, vegetation is vegetation. Don't let different vegetation like palm trees for instance rob you of the joy you could have at your local beach where there are possibly only simple trees. An island? Whether you are on an island or not, you wouldn't notice. Now I am not saying that some places might be more beautiful than others, but did we ever take the time to appreciate the ones that we do afford to go to, or are we obsessing about what other people have, thus blinding ourselves from the beauties we do possess?

Imagine the person you wish to become and take measures to fulfil that dream. Having more wealth, possession and all things similar might be fun, but it is often not up to us. Favourable or unfavourable events happen in our life, uncontrollably, and we often cannot influence these events. But, what we can influence is our reaction to them, and the possibility to create our own life-changing events. So don't work on achieving material goods, rather work on yourself. Get stronger, both mentally and physically, the rest might follow afterwards.

The distance between you and a better life, with more wealth, health, energy, fresh air and without an unpleasant stench is just a few days. In each moment of your life as a smoker, you have been only a few days away from all these. And you would get closer to them each second, and farther away with each cigarette, even with each puff. You never really allowed yourself to succeed in life. Smoking has always pulled you down, and I bet that by now you can see this on your own. One day is left, and a new life begins. If you feel any form of anxiety, take some time tonight and ponder about all that you have read, about all that smoking suppressed in life for you and on all the greatness that awaits. One more day.

DAY -1

Tomorrow is the big day. Try planning ahead for it, starting today: what work to you have to do tomorrow, do you have any events planned? Try making it a busy day, if nothing special happens, add fillers to it. Try not doing anything stressful or soliciting. Just keep yourself busy with various tasks and activities so you won't have any time to think about smoking.

In this evening, if you will still have a few cigarettes, throw them away. Even better, rip them apart so you won't be tempted to look for them in the garbage (been there). Don't smoke your last cigarette with the sadness of a "breakup", rather with the joy of ending this torment and starting a new, healthier, cleaner and better life. While you smoke your last cigarette, try to feel one last time how it slowly destroys you, how the smoke enters your lungs while charring its walls, how the toxins enter your bloodstream thus making you feel uneasy and unwell. Think about all the chemicals you inhale. After finishing it, try feeling joy by the thought of starting your life as a non-smoker.

I suggest that your last cigarette shouldn't be right before going to bed. Smoke it before 7 PM and use the rest of your evening to think about the life you will lead now that you are free. Finally, you won't have to hide while smoking or you won't have to worry that you don't have money to buy a new pack or anything else that comes to mind.

Try doing a lot of physical exercise today. If you still do not have a gym subscription, and neither did you start jogging, I urge you to start now. Sweat so you can eliminate toxins and so that you may learn to breathe air. As funny as this sounds, we as smokers forget how to breathe in and enjoy the air. Also, when cravings appear you might feel like you aren't receiving enough air. In those moments, it is best to breathe in deeply and in the blink of an eye, the cravings will dissipate.

In case you haven't told your friends about your intentions yet, do it now. This has to be done so you won't find yourself surrounded by them smoking and offering you cigarettes. They might not even take your decision seriously and would try to persuade you to continue smoking. As I said, if they would praise you for quitting, they would have to admit that what they are doing is wrong, and our ego surely doesn't like us admitting we're wrong. But tell them about your decision especially so that they can help and support you. If you have the courage, post on a social media network about your intention to quit. Write a post that everybody can see and tell them that tomorrow you are going to start a new life, as a non-smoker, and ask everyone to support you morally, but even physically whenever you are next to them and feel uneasy by any possible cravings. By doing such a public statement, you are applying pressure to yourself and you won't want to break your word. Since everyone saw your intentions, it would be a pity to make a fool of yourself by continuing to smoke. Go all in. I know, pressure and stress surely isn't good, especially when they might lead to cravings, but in this case it is a constructive pressure. You won't smoke anymore, so it doesn't really affect you if you do make this statement, right? Trust me, everybody will support and root for you. They will understand and respect the decision you have taken and they won't tempt you (unless they are enemies in disguise), but on the contrary. Maybe they will stop smoking in front of you, for your sake, or at least they will scold you if you try to give in.

Come on, do it now. Not later. Take this spontaneous decision right now. I will help you with some ideas. You can do a similar statement to the one I wrote below, or one conceived by yourself:

"I am a non-smoker now. I am very happy and elated about my new choice. I already feel positive changes in my mind and body. I will be firm with the decision I took and I will resist any temptation. However, the first days and weeks will be hard. I will possibly be irritable, apathetic, aggressive, nervous or indifferent. It won't be easy for me, but I will consciously fight against any obstacles I might face and I need your help. Here is how you can help me:

- Don't call me to smoke and don't smoke around me, at least for a few days;
- Don't offer me cigarettes, not even as a joke. If I ask you for some, don't give me any and tell me

to remember why I made this decision. I have a long list of reasons;
- Don't judge me when I ask telling you what I am going through. Support me;

If I am stressed while out or at a party and I ask you to give me a puff:
- Please don't give me any;
- Try to convince me that the need to smoke is temporary and if I am strong enough now, it will pass quickly;
- Remind me that I made the right decision to stop smoking;
- Distract my attention from smoking, verbally or with an activity.

I am sure I will succeed with your help!

If you have posted this statement, or a similar one, I will assure you that you have made a right choice. Through the act of writing it down and making it public, you are strengthening the decision in your subconscious. It will feel helpless and will start supporting this change in lifestyle so that you won't make a fool of yourself in front of others if you give in to smoking.

Think about how much time it would take until you will be completely "healed" from the disease of smoking. Don't expect a day or two, rather be realistic. The time may vary from person to person, and if tomorrow or the day after that you will still experience cravings, don't panic, it's normal and they will pass as fast as they appeared. Don't even think for a moment that it is too hard and you won't make it. You will. All fresh non-smokers go through the same thing and think the same. Prepare yourself spiritually for what will follow. Don't be tempted to imagine that you won't feel a thing, but don't let yourself be terrified either, because, honestly, you are stronger than any temptation there is. Any cravings that might appear will last for such a low amount of time that you won't even notice them. But you could amplify them by feeding them with fear, anxiety and negative thoughts. Without these "fuels", they will be inoffensive and will vanish as fast as they appeared.

This is it for today. Go to bed with a smile on your face, tomorrow a new life starts, one that you long deserved. You will rise from the "ashes" and you will be born a new man.

+ 7 DAYS

You have finally made it! Now you are a non-smoker, congratulations! Or, if you aren't one yet, I salute you for your ambition in getting so far and for at least trying to be receptive to the information I have presented. I encourage you to act upon everything you have learned so far and to start the process of becoming a non-smoker. I have succeeded, others have too, and so will you. Persistence is key, the rest comes by itself. So it can be easier for you; in the next pages I will describe the first seven days of my life as a non-smoker, extracted from my personal journal. I have added some extra ideas to them that will help you fight the need for tobacco and to ward off withdrawal. I have written this journal so I can keep my mind busy during those days and to notice what triggered me into smoking so that I may be able to solve them the next time I try, if I fail.

The good news is that I didn't give in to smoking. I haven't smoked since. I followed the steps I have described in this book, I have endured withdrawal symptoms, I understood where they came from and thus I managed to fight them. With an iron will, I became a non-smoker, and remained one. Now I am sharing my experience with you. I admit the first days were hard, but not impossible, and not nearly hard enough for me to give in and continue ruining my life. Take note, I didn't have this book handy to help me, but I created and perfected it so that you do.

Reading about my experience could help you learn from them and face temptation. Applying what you have thus learned and what you are yet to read will help you in the upcoming days. Read them any time you are in danger of giving in to temptation, all at once or at least one per day. But read them so you can keep your mind busy and that you don't feel like fighting this battle alone. Withdrawal can manifest itself different from person to person and our daily routines may vary, so be creative and adapt yourself to what I have written. I have promised you at the beginning of this book that I will be along your side, and I will remain so any time you need too, through these words.

We will become non-smokers now together. Together we will go through this pain day by day. We are like two friends that support each other into quitting. You can understand what I went through in my first days as a non-smoker and you will see it isn't as hard as you may have imagined. Soon enough, you will have a cleansed body, more money, energy, health and success.

I recommend you log your own days. Keep a journal and write down how you experience withdrawal, how you plan on fighting it in the future days. Try to figure out what triggers you to smoke so that you may avoid them in the following days. Analyze the moments that you feel cravings are at their peak, and why. Maybe you were simply thirsty, as I said, dehydration can be mistaken as a tobacco craving. Share this newly found information with a close person and ask them to help you during this period of time.

From my experience, and after a lot of study, I can tell you that there is no magical word I can utter for you to suddenly quit smoking without withdrawal or the need to smoke. Likewise, there is no simply technique, like saying for 40 time "Ave Maria" and making seven crosses. Actually, the whole book is rather such a technique. The sum of the information, advice and instruction that reside in this book are the final method through which you can become a non-smoker. I have followed them all and have concentrated them into this book, especially for you, so you may be able to embrace the new life of a non-smoker with great ease.

Apply the techniques I personally used in the following days. Add your own ideas to them. Our lives are different, our daily experiences vary and that is why maybe you need a different approach to defeat any obstacles that might appear. Be creative and inspire yourself from my own experience.

Many smokers fail while they attempt to quit smoking because they feel that something bad is going to happen once they do so. They ask themselves if they will ever experience life the same as they did while smoking. Will they still be happy, they might ask themselves. If you didn't manage to quit smoking yet, insist on changing your mentality and perception regarding cigarettes. Become a non-smoker with a sense of joy, enthusiasm and relief, not terror. Be conscious that from now on you will interact with other people better, you will be firm on dealing with stress and challenges and you won't be addicted to cigarettes anymore. From the amount of energy and heath you will receive, it will be impossible for you not to excel.

Look at other smokers not with envy but rather with pity. You realize that they light up their cigarettes only because they can't have the same feeling of relaxation and relief a non-smoker enjoys. The only thing that prevents them from leading such a relaxed living is the last dose of nicotine they have received and the anticipation of the next dose.

Life is easy and beautiful, but we tend to complicate it. If you can see the general picture of things, if you perceive life as an infinite matrix of constants represented by people, habits, events and circumstances and if you notice the patterns that are found everywhere in the human behavior and nature, if you can understand them, then you won't perceive life as a random chain of events anymore, but you will create your own future, through simple, concrete actions. Each day will be a reason for you to enjoy life, to think positively. New opportunities that you will manage with success will arise.

It is very important you understand that you, and only you, own control over your life. Lots of people constantly complain, but only few of them are able to make a change. It's all up to you. But you have to be able to constantly develop yourself, to invest in yourself, in your education. You can't reach your goals until you invest in your own mind so that you may be able to understand it and control it. Invest time in yourself, meditate and get to know the person you are better and try visualising what you can become. You would be surprised to find that you know little about your actual self as you might live an inertia driven life, instead of one you have control upon. At the right time, you will be able to achieve anything you can imagine. Your mind will transform any positive things, through your eyes, in reality, thus you will start seeing everything by its positive side. The future belongs only to those who are able to believe in the beauty of their dreams, and currently, your biggest dream should be to become a non-smoker.

I will provide a short list of things you can do if you experience withdrawal on any day:

- Go for a few minute long walk with someone you can talk you so that they may distract you from any thought of smoking;
- Do a bit of gymnastics: abs, pushups, squats. The desire to smoke will pass on quickly and the decision to do sudden physical exercise will re-vitalize you. If you live in a flat or have stairs at your workplace, try going up and down them

a few times. Once is enough to remove any cravings you might feel and you will oxygenize your brain for an extra energy boost;

- Fill your time with all sorts of activities. Clean up, groom yourself, polish your shoes, read;
- Meditate upon your goals. A good breath will help you release dopamine and it can give you an impulse of energy;
- Drink water anytime you might experience cravings, you might confuse hunger or thirst with nicotine addiction;
- Keep your mouth and hand busy with a toothpick, a pen or sugarless chewing-gum;
- Eat or slowly chew on i.e. nuts;
- Inhale deeply and exhale all the air from your lungs. Replace the needs to smoke with the need for air and repeat in your mind or out loud: "I need air, I will offer myself air";

Let's start! Great and wonderful things are just around the corner and there is no purpose in postponing. Maybe you can't see or feel them, but they are there. Quit smoking, now or never.

Day + 1

Welcome to your first day as a non-smoker. Don't be afraid, it isn't and it won't be hard as long as you don't allow anyone or any event to affect your situation.

The reason we don't achieve any progress and we don't want to make any changes, like becoming a non-smoker or doing physical exercise, being more peaceful and to behave nicer to people, is that we cling on to our ego too much, to our personality, to who we are. If we try accepting change, we feel like we are leaving aside who we are to become someone else. Thus, our mind enters a state of conflict with the idea of abandoning ones to become something else. It feels as if it is dying. However, you have already changed. You already are a different person. From the moment you began reading this book, you started a reforming process, and at this point you are closer to becoming what you wish to be. Persist and you will succeed.

We are conservative beings. We like routine and order. We need a stable ego. That is why change is best if made gradually. We have to focus on doing small steps towards our goals, daily. These small changes will add up over time and will bear impressive results. We are complex creatures with little free time, which is why we can't handle shocks or sudden changes. Small steps taken slowly and careful will be the foundation of what we desire to become. Until today, you have made such small steps towards improving many aspects of your life and to get rid of smoking. The changes didn't happen overnight. Now, as a non-smoker, you can focus on other positive changes that may improve your life, but I recommend you continue applying them progressively, not all at once. Focus on adapting yourself to a non-smoker life. It is a major transformation and it requires a lot of attention from your side. Do not fight on multiple fronts simultaneously, but use the power of your mind to focus on the current battle-field.

Chance made my first day as a non-smoker to be on a Monday. I didn't pick it on purpose and I can tell you if I were to start over, I wouldn't pick any other day just because Mondays are considered to be the hardest days of the week.

After the first 30 minutes up to the next 4 hours, the effects of nicotine begin to diminish and your cravings will follow suit. After 10 hours, you will feel restless and the physical cravings will intensify. Anxiety can intervene.

In the following days try to avoid negative emotions and feelings. Watch funny and relaxing movies, spend your time with happy people that cheer you up. You don't need to deal with anxiety and general frustration during this time period. They could worsen your withdrawal and cravings. What pulls you down? What makes you enter a state of melancholy or anxiety, disabling you to progress? Can you avoid such events, one way or another, in the next period of time? Try leaving toxic relationships with other people aside – I mean friends that influence you negatively.

Maybe you pull yourself down. Look in the mirror and ask yourself: what am I doing? Why am I looking for excuses to smoke when I could lead a happy life? Why am I engaging in self-destructive behavior? The sooner you get honest with yourself and find out why you keep looking for excuses to smoke, the sooner you will be able to handle the reasons and move on. Instead of wasting your energy and thoughts on reasons to smoke, re-orient yourself on a set of actions you have to take to get control over your life back.

Predictable success is the result of a good programming of the brain so that you may be able to think, feel and do what is necessary for you to reach your goals. Remind yourself that you are at charge and do whatever is necessary for you to obtain what you truly desire: to become a non-smoker. If you haven't yet succeeded in convincing your subconscious that you want to quit, it isn't too late. You can even do it in the moments in which you feel that your mind tries to persuade you to smoke. As it is the first day, it won't be too hard. Furthermore, it's a good occasion to exercise your willpower.

Try practicing the breathing exercise I was talking about in an earlier chapter. If you feel the acute need to smoke, tell yourself that you actually feel the need to breath in deeply, the need for air. Inhale deeply and imagine that you are giving yourself what you desire. More air. You always need air. High levels of carbon monoxide in your blood is correlated to anxiety. You already know that, while you were smoking, you allowed carbon monoxide to enter the bloodstream. So, if you are stressed out, a cigarette won't help you for more than a few minutes while lessening withdrawal. After the dopamine effects pass, you will feel how the cigarette actually amplified your anxiety or stress. Inhale deeply and exhale all the air from your lungs so you may remove the extra carbon monoxide from your blood.

Maybe you are a social being who likes to go out often. But remember, now you are trying to do a major change in good so you can sacrifice your social life for the next couple of weeks especially if there are smokers in your social circle. You don't have to expose yourself to possible reasons for temptation during this period of time. If you find yourself in such a situation and feel like you can't handle it, go home. Your health and life are at play and you don't want to sacrifice them for a few extra moments in which you could give in to smoking.

In this day I started saving money the money I would usually spend on cigarettes. I put them in a jar. I recommend you do the same. After a month as a non-smoker treat yourself with that money. Buy something, anything you like. A gift, a reward for your victory. You can calculate in advance how much money you were used to spend per month and thus you can make a general idea of the amount of money you will save. Think about what you can buy with that money. If the sum isn't too big, at least have a massage or go to a relaxing spa.

Your first day should pass by easily. The subconscious isn't yet aware of your plans and it probably considers the fact that you didn't smoke today exceptional. If you didn't listen to the advice in "-7 Days" and have smoked a lot of cigarettes the previous day, then your subconscious will understand what you are doing later on in the afternoon up to the evening. But it will be too late, you are probably already at home, without cigarettes, and hopefully not alone.

Our target when we face the absence of nicotine is to experiment on new ways of putting our life in order. A new life can be stressful and often accompanied by anxiety. If we admit that stress and anxiety are part of the natural healing process of our body, that they are a means for the change in good and that nothing is wrong with us, we will progress easier.

If you start experiencing cravings think about what determines you to smoke, what triggers provide cravings and the feeling of emptiness in life. When you wake up, when you drink your coffee, when you fight with someone, when you go out, when you drink alcohol? Try finding substitutes to all of these situations. I am not saying you shouldn't participate in social events, but, once you arrive at them, don't think about the fact that you no longer smoke. In example, if a group walks out of a bar to smoke and you are left behind, alone, you can call a friend or a loved one to keep you company and distract your attention until the smokers return. Many people hold a tooth-pick or a pen in their hand and mouth instead of a cigarette. This way they manage to fool the mind and replace the action of bringing the cigarette to the mouth. Maybe you look ridiculous with a tooth-pick in your mouth at social events, but in those specific moments you can rely on sugarless chewing-gum. Mint inhibits cravings and it keeps your mouth and mind busy with chewing.

Imagine scenarios before going out. What persons are you about to meet, if they are smokers or not. If they are non-smokers, it is alright, simply ask them to keep an eye on you so you won't buy any cigarettes and ask them to distract you whenever you feel restless. Plan ahead before a possible event in which you might be tempted to smoke unfolds. This way you won't get surprised by triggers and you will manage to avoid them. Try not to allow situations in which you have to choose between smoking or enduring cravings for the rest of the night to appear. It will be more difficult to resist temptation on the spot rather than anticipating it.

The days that follow should be well organized so you know exactly what you are going to do and how. To avoid a chaotic day, one that could go out of control and provide you anxiety and cravings, write a list of what you have to do the next day, or even the whole week. Estimate how much time it would take you to realize those tasks and think about how you are going to finish them. Don't leave any empty spaces in your schedule. These voids in your daily routine can be easily filled by the subconscious with cravings. If you manage to fill out your days, but sudden unexpected events appear into your schedule, don't alarm yourself. Try carrying out only the important tasks in your schedule and remove the ones you used as fillers or use them for the upcoming week. Currently, our main priority is to keep you busy and far away from the toxins found in cigarettes.

The list shouldn't be long, otherwise you may feel overwhelmed. In principle, write down tasks that may gradually improve your lifestyle, like rearranging your desktop, cleaning your wardrobe, your drawer, reading, and physical exercise – tasks that you can easily leave aside if more important, unforeseeable events may occur.

In this list, you can include two types of, progress brining, activities: things that you need to do and things that you want to do. The more activities that need to be done you accomplish, the sooner they will transform in in activities that you want to do. You receive dopamine through their accomplishment and your body will start craving dopamine that is released from such activities. This is because, through such repetition, you train your subconscious into accepting them as part of your necessary lifestyle. However, if you start doing only activities that need to be done, you get tired, so it is better that from time to time you orient yourself into doing things you like too. That is why I recommend you write in your list daily tasks and activities which you consider are a great joy for yourself and help you evolve.

DAY +2

In this morning I have confronted the need to smoke. In the first day I didn't feel a thing in the morning. My body still had some nicotine reserves from the previous day, but by now they were depleted. My mind probably thought yesterday that I simply had a busy day and I was really unable to smoke. However, this morning it noticed something unusual: although I did have more time, I didn't engage in smoking. When I noticed it wouldn't stop nagging me, I started repeating positive affirmations like: "I am a non-smoker now and I feel great", "I have waited this moment for a long time, and now I am finally free". Repeat these sentences out loud or in your mind as often you can. The mind won't support you in your fight against cravings unless you make it understand that this is your purpose, your intention. If the subconscious will start "scaring" you with cravings and thoughts that you won't succeed, explain to it, through such affirmations, that everything goes according to plan, nothing bad will happen and you are truly happy with this new life.

Don't forget that the desire to smoke can appear at any moment. The brain has its own efficient tricks to persuade your conscious mind that a cigarette won't do you any harm. Remember, you have thought it for several years with reasons and excuses to smoke, so it will act accordingly. Heed my word, a single cigarette can do more harm than you can imagine. It will ruin everything you have planned and prepared so far and it will cancel your motivation out. So don't light it up.

Notice that nicotine cravings are caused by the last cigarette you smoked. Each time you are going to light a new one up, you will have to go through the same feelings and cravings again. But with each second and hour you abstain, you will defeat these inner demons and you will get closer to freedom. As you succeed in resisting a craving, the next one will be weaker, and so on until it doesn't exist anymore. Anyone can quit smoking, even you. Try printing this into your mind if you feel things get hard for you. Remind yourself that who didn't succeed in quitting smoking didn't really try doing so.

Before I became a non-smoker I have read that a lot of people experience insomnia due to nicotine withdrawal. I found that this in true in some measure. Insomnia is caused by the surplus of energy and mental acuity you will receive through the new and healthy lifestyle of a toxin-free non-smoker. I can tell you that things are going to settle down in a few days and your sleeping habits will get back to normal. But until then you might need some rest and a good night's sleep so you may be able to get your work done without anxiety showing up and making cravings worse. Try taking some melatonin or other natural based sedatives. Melatonin is a hormone that is produced by the pineal gland and helps the body sleep. The body produces a lot of melatonin at night, when it is dark, and it is removed from the body with natural light. However, before using melatonin or any other natural supplement, talk to a doctor.

I know I should talk more about how to keep yourself from smoking, but I can't help myself from digressions. I am very enthusiastic about the fact that you can rectify your life on other ways as well. While working on staying a non-smoker and integrating into your new life, you will have the great benefit of improving your willpower and motivation. Due to these, the money you save and the freshly acquired energy, you will do wonders. You will finally be able to develop your physique and have the body you have always desired. As you will no longer smoke, you will focus on conversations while out in society instead of the gesture of smoking. Thus you will surely develop your charisma while paying more attention to other people and leaving room for new business opportunities. Make a hobby out of this. Get actively involved in conversations and truly listen to what others have to say. This way you will keep your mind active instead of numbing it down with smoking. You will gradually become a person in which in the best you could only look up to.

I challenge you to write a story about yourself. How you would see yourself in a year, what person you would wish to be. Describe your ideal life and person and how you would like things to unfold. When done, start acting in ways that will lead you to that imagined life. Aim for realistic goals. Don't imagine yourself on a yacht if you really are physically far away from that possibility, but rather try seeking joy wherever you find yourself through the things you can do with your surroundings. If in the process you manage to arrive on that yacht, good for you. Behave as if the world belongs to you. This imaginative game will help you in the following days in which you might experience withdrawal. By thinking about who and what you could become, mere thoughts of cigarettes will fade away and your mind will focus on the dreams you have created. Imagine a beautiful life and your mind will begin to conspire towards materialising it while realizing that smoking actually jeopardizes the dream. You won't feel any withdrawal anymore for smoking, but for moments when you are harming the possibility of achieving your dreams. Therefore, the only measures you will take to diminish this "withdrawal" are the ones necessary for personal growth.

This day has passed well for me. At about 5 pm, after work, I went to the grocery store to do some shopping. Everything was fine, but at a certain point I started feeling big cravings. I remembered what I have learned and I analysed the reason for which this craving might have appeared. I noticed that I was experiencing it due to the fact that I was actually thirsty. I was confusing thirst with an intense need to smoke, so I opened a bottle of water and I started drinking. Surprisingly, the cravings disappeared instantly and I continued shopping like I hadn't felt them in the first place. I found this situation often in the following days. I used to confuse hunger or thirst with nicotine cravings. That is why, I advise you to always keep water handy and something healthy to snack on.

DAY +3

There shouldn't be any trace of nicotine left in your body anymore after three days. The withdrawal and the need for smoking diminish, but it is possible that anxiety might step in.

I noticed that, while I was smoking, I have suffered from withdrawal especially if I wasn't smoking for a few hours. I was always looking for moments to smoke and if they didn't appear it would be hard for me. Now that I know that I am no longer smoking, I don't even think about it anymore and the mind seems to stop nagging me to smoke because of this. Whenever I remember about the existence of cigarettes I do feel a small need to smoke, but small enough that any other distraction would make me forget about them. These are the body and mind's last futile attempts to convince me to smoke. Ant his only because I didn't have such a book to help me, like you do, with all the information gathered at one place. The information resides only in my mind and I would use it only when and if I remembered them. You have the advantage of having it handy and being able to read any chapter you need whenever necessary.

Make always use of everything you have learned through this book and your own personal experience. Not only will they help you get over cravings easier (or even experiencing them at all) but you won't start smoking again and you will never wish to do so at all. It is possible that, after a while, you consider yourself strong enough and you start negotiating that you may smoke a cigarette to once again convince yourself that it doesn't taste good and that it doesn't make you feel better. You might think that this will help your cause and surely convince you to continue remaining a non-smoker. Don't fall into this self-conceived trap. The subconscious, masked in ambition, will try to fool you. Once you start smoking your body gets addicted to nicotine and you will have to go through all this hassle from the beginning.

Be grateful to what you have. It will make you feel better and it will help you accept your situation. We are always stressed out from various circumstances. We see how others enjoy success while we struggle to play our rent. Therefore, we end up seeking other peoples' lives instead of realising that we have a wonderful life ourselves, a beautiful family and our own dreams to which realisation we can work upon. We let ourselves be blinded by the success of other people, therefore we begin to envy them and hate our own existence when it would be enough to accept ourselves for who we are and manage to reach our ideals. Wasting energy with hateful feelings towards the "haves" of others simply blinds us from the progress we ourselves can achieve, thus rendering us unable to act upon our life.

Assign time for meditation and think about what you can be grateful for. Even if your life isn't as you wished it would be, I am sure you have lots of reasons to be thankful for. When you are grateful, a positive vibe emits from your body. This feeling will uplift you and due it you will face any obstacles with great ease. Be happy with what you have so you can focus your energy towards building a better life, rather than envying one others life. Negative thoughts shake the foundation of your self-confidence and it will be hard for you to progress, especially if you have the impression that up until now, everything you did was in vain and meaningless. Stop considering that you won't bring any benefit into your life regardless of what you do. You have brought and you will continue to do so. Gratitude for what you already have and the fact that you are still alive are the building blocks of a bright future.

In my third night as a non-smoker, I went out to a wine tasting. Usually, I wouldn't have participated but it was done by close friends and I went there to support them. It was easy for me, no cravings appeared and the time passed by quickly. I didn't feel any withdrawal symptoms or cravings even though I consumed alcohol. As it is not allowed to smoke inside places, the absence of cigarettes didn't bother me. I managed to resist for a full three hours without even thinking of smoking. I must admit, after the event, someone said they would go out to smoke and then suddenly some cravings appeared. Until then I didn't feel a thing but the mere thought of someone smoking while I couldn't induced withdrawal. It didn't last long though, as I was sitting at a table with friends because they distracted my attention. I then realised that I can have fun, interact with others and engage in conversations even without smoking. It was raining outside that night and I could only feel pity for the ones out there, soaked wet and with tar-heavy lungs. This way, I held an inner monologue with my subconscious and I made it understand that I am ready to embrace this new life, that I am adapting well, while pleading for its support. Slowly, it started understanding and accepting the fact that I am not a non-smoker. After a short while, it started aiding me by removing the old triggers.

Day +4

Some claim that due to withdrawal symptoms they are tired and unable to finish their tasks, unable to think straight, thus falling prey to anxiety which worsens their situation. All I can say it that they didn't fully understand how the body and mind works related to nicotine. You understand these facts, so you won't be experiencing such unpleasant situations. If however you will have withdrawal and you didn't manage to persuade your subconscious that it is better to live a non-smoker life, try approaching the problem from a different angle. Do cold showers. I know, lots of people talk about this and it is already irritating. Cold showers are unpleasant, especially during winter. But at least try to reduce the water temperature. It will improve your blood flow and once the cold water hits your skin you will begin inhaling more deeply. Therefore, the carbon monoxide levels inside your blood decease while diminishing stress and anxiety. The feeling of cold water on your skin will make the blood head towards the internal organs, fuelling them and optimizing their operating mechanism while supporting your metabolic rate and reinvigorating you. If you do such a cold shower in the morning you will receive a wave of adrenaline that will stimulate you throughout the day and you can start solving your small tasks quickly. By solving them, dopamine will be released and it will help you face the major problems of the day, like possible withdrawal. Like the butterfly effect, such a small and seemingly meaningless action can lead to great, unexpected results. This is why I have always promoted you should do things actively, consciously, so that you may foresee such possible chain events.

I must confess: I often felt the desire to smoke, at least for a puff, but during the first two or three days. I didn't give into these cravings though. This acute need to smoke usually dissipated after 10 minutes – I knew and accepted the fact that I had to go through them to reach my end goal – so I left it do its thing, knowing that greater things would await if I was strong enough in those moments. After the cravings passed, I was amazed of how well I felt. I simply didn't want or had the need to smoke. This empowered me to resist other cravings, knowing that once they pass, I can resume whatever I was doing. When I went out with my friends and they'd go smoking, I would join them but I wouldn't smoke and I avoided the smoke. I would instead listen to what they had to say and engage in the conversation. My mind was this busy talking and in those four to five minutes my friends would spend on smoking I'd play with a bottle-cap or a plastic spoon to keep my hands busy and distract myself. Through this method I was able to stay with them without intoxicating myself.

If I remember correctly, in my previous attempts to quit smoking everything worked smoothly and I wished to push my limits, so I would go out with friends and have a drink. That wasn't a really good idea since alcohol made me relapse. Then I'd get demoralised and I wouldn't attempt in quitting for a long period of time. But this time I was informed regarding smoking and I knew how to control my cravings. I consumed alcohol on various occasions this week and I didn't feel strong urges to smoke. However, I don't recommend you do the same. Maybe you aren't as prepared as I was and it isn't good too test your limits, not now at least as you may risk in giving in and that would throw your whole plan away. If you can, go out with non-smokers or your loved one and ask them to keep an eye on you.

In this evening I went out with my friends. One of them is about to get married so we kind of went to a bachelor party. We were three, the other two were smokers. I was tempted to smoke a few times myself, I won't lie. But the urges were merely on a psychological level, and even minor ones. Physically I did not feel the need for nicotine; the smell of cigarette smoke was rather unappealing so I was trying to wary away from smoke. Psychologically I felt like I would like to participate in the action that my friends were engaged in, smoking I mean. I felt like being excluded because I wouldn't smoke. When I realised that my subconscious was urging me to smoke, and that it was the reason I felt excluded, I gave it what it desired, in a way. Each time I saw someone puff a cigarette, I would take a sip of the drink I was holding in my hand. Thereby, I was doing the hand to mouth gesture that was embedded into my psyche without intoxicating myself with burnt tobacco. I did it without really focusing on the task at hand and while participating in whatever we talked about. I can honestly tell you that this trick worked and I didn't feel the slightest need to smoke anymore.

As I said countless times, it is very easy to become a non-smoker once you truly wish to be one and once you understand why you act the way you do. Analysing your behaviour, your mind and your biological needs, you will realise why you engage in smoking, but also how to proceed in stopping this vice.

DAY +5

I used to smoke a lot at work. I was always

alone, working on my laptop, in my own office, but sometimes I also had to do physical work. I smoked continuously. I would light up a cigarette after another without me even noticing. To be able to fulfil my physical tasks, I had to get off my chair, but as I constantly had a cigarette in my hand, I always postpone my task until after I finish smoking. But I would light another up, and then another. Sometimes I would even sit and look at the blank screen so I could finish smoking, only so I could light another one up out of habit. I didn't get far in finishing my tasks this way and they would pile up, causing my anxiety, which made me engage in the compulsive behaviour of smoking once again. A vicious cycle was entered once again. Now that I am no longer tied up to my desk and ashtray I have noticed that I am a lot more efficient. If I need something to be done I simply get off my chair and solve the problem. My efficiency rose surprisingly much, I managed to get my work done a lot faster and I managed to spare a lot of time that I used to for self-development. I do more physical exercise at my workplace since the air is now breathable, I read more or I simply have more time to look for new business ideas or how to grow my current one.

In the evening of my fifth day as a non-smoker, I went out again. I am part of a NGO called Rotary. I know this might seem like I am inventing the events mentioned in these days for the sake of writing this book or that I have intentionally picked such a challenging week, but as I said earlier in this book, there will never be a good moment to quit smoking. There is always something that might come up and that is why you simply have to take the decision to quit whatever day or week it is.

Rotary in my hometown has meetings each week. Up until now I would smoke a cigarette each time before the meeting would begin, outside, either alone or with fellow members. In my luck, not every member smokes, so now I could stay inside with the other non-smokers and I wouldn't feel excluded. The idea is not to expose yourself to smoke and not to confuse the vice with desire, but consider it an action you don't want to participate in. If the others, instead of smoking, would jump on one leg, would you jump too or would you find it ridiculous? You can relate this to smoking; the act has value only if you offer it and just because others do it, doesn't make it right. Its real value, without question, is negative.

It is time to remind everybody that you are a non-smoker now and to ask for their further support. Tell them how many days you are smoke-free. They will congratulate you and be proud of you. Absorb all this praise and let it fuel your motivation to continue. Try realising that there is no way back. If you were to start smoking again, you would disappoint everybody and you would prove your incapability and lack of perseverance.

Tell others that you are willing to help them quit smoking, with your own experience. Many will actually be thrilled by the idea and thank you. If you think this book has helped you, please recommend it.

What techniques have helped you so far to resist smoking and temptation? Write them down so you can have them handy in any critical circumstance that might appear. You didn't write anything down yet? No problem, you can start doing so right now to avoid unforeseeable and tempting events. Since it is your fifth day as a non-smoker you surely have acquired a lot of extra time to do such a list, or any kind of list I have mentioned before in this book. Don't believe that the hard part has passed, you can never know what your mind plots to make you smoke again. It might be waiting for the right moment, for you to be drunk or maybe a strong trigger to arise. Be prepared, always.

Remember how hard it was at the beginning to resist temptation and how easy it is now? I promised that the cravings will lose strength over time and now you can surely notice I was right. If you feel the need to smoke, it surely is a week feeling and it will get even weaker over time with each time you resist. Don't surrender to your impulse to smoke, otherwise you would have to start all over again and you will prolong your torment. Accept the idea that you are now a non-smoker.

Don't fall in traps that temptation might set. The best ideas and reasons to smoke come up when you are attempting to quit. You might tell yourself that there are various events in which you absolutely **must** smoke otherwise you are unable to handle them. You might tell yourself that you can light one up so you can convince yourself that it doesn't taste well. I can tell you that you are wasting your imagination and energy with finding reasons to smoke. There are no real ones, only the ones we lie ourselves with. In those moments you surrender control to your subconscious which will grind you up with fear and doubt until it will convince you to smoke again. Fight it off with your conscious mind, with powerful, positive affirmations and the idea that your life has improved and it is heading towards perfection. What is this perfection you might ask? Well, it is being the best you can be with whatever resources you have. The perception of perfection varies from person to person, but in the end, it means being happy and feeling fulfilled with what you have.

DAY +6

I knew, even before these seven days, that on the sixth day of my life as a non-smoker I would attend a wedding of a close friend. Being a close friend with the groom, I was telling myself that probably I would participate at the wedding for more time than I usually would, but without cigarettes I would have any fun. Time would pass by very slow I thought and I would suffer terribly from withdrawal instead of enjoying myself. I admit that I thought for a lot of time that I wouldn't have fun and I was tempted to shift quitting to next week. But I didn't. I faced my fears, learned that I can have fun even without cigarettes and so I managed to succeed and adapt to my new life.

Urges to smoke did come up, I won't deny it. In the previous days not so much, but this night I ate a lot, way more then I should have, I drank lots of coffee and alcohol. Many of my smoker friends were present. But I wasn't alone and I would stay inside, with non-smokers. The idea is persist because then you can resist and do anything. The wedding was beautiful. I danced with my loved one, I talked with my non-smoker friends inside and I would even go outside with my friends that did smoke. Whether I felt cravings or not was irrelevant, I still had a fun time. As my olfactory sense almost completely recovered, I started detesting the smell of smoke that resided even on the clothes of the people inside. My cravings were mere psychological, but once I felt this disgust they would cease to exist. Honestly I didn't imagine that this evening would pass by so easily and that I could have fun without smoking and without thinking about cigarettes too much. I hereby learned that you shouldn't declare something impossible until you actually try to realise it.

Cigarette cravings don't mean that your body actually requires nicotine, and neither the cravings nor the emotions associated with them will last for long. Let them pass by, they are part of the process of becoming a non-smoker. Most ex-smokers went through them and managed to overcome them. So will you. Don't try to change them; don't judge yourself for having them. It's like going to the dentist, it might hurt but you have to withstand the pain, otherwise the caries will get bigger. Endure and don't react to the cravings or otherwise they might intensify. They will surely pass faster than you expect. The temptation to smoke is different from the feeling of hunger. You are hungry, and then you get more hungry, then you get sick from the hunger, especially because it actually is a necessity to eat. The need to smoke lessens, because you don't really need to smoke to survive. The body heals itself and it will then heal you from this obsession regarding cigarettes slowly. You just have to hang in there for a few days, after which you can start enjoying the dozens of benefits of being a non-smoker.

I noticed that by respecting the seven preparatory days, it is easier to become a non-smoker. There were no big and unbearable cravings present. The only thing that conspired against me was my own mind. I didn't feel intense withdrawal but my mind kept reminding me of the possibility to smoke on various occasions. Either in trying doing so in the morning, with the excuse that one cigarette would last me for the rest of the day and I wouldn't have to smoke more, either to make the time pass faster when I was bored. In neither cases did I actually experience a physical need to smoke.

Day +7

You finally made it to your seventh day as a non-smoker! All I can say is: congratulations! I am proud of you and I am sure that the ones that care for you are aswell. Everybody believed in you and now you are proving them that you do have the will to accomplish your dream of becoming a non-smoker and anything else in life. Maybe you don't realise but you are truly worthy of appreciation at this point. Cigarettes only pulled you down, but now since you unshackled yourself from this vice, you are free to run towards your goals! The rays of glory start enlightening your life and soon enough, with a little more effort, you can start building upon your life as you truly wished it would be.

Allow yourself today a few moments of reflection. Lie down on your bed and think about how well you have handled your life as a non-smoker so far. You have made a major change for the good in your life. Victory is at your grasp. You have made it to the seventh day without smoking and I can assure you that the chances of relapse are pretty slim now, as long as you continue to actively apply what techniques you used in order to withstand cravings this week.

Visualize the change in your life. How well you feel now, how much extra energy and time you possess. I bet the savings from this week look pretty great too. The sum might not be big, but it will grow and you can treat yourself after the month is over.

On top of that, the savings are extra money you wouldn't of have had anyways. Think about the negative aspects of smoking. You would stay out whether it was cold, raining or hot. Maybe you had to smoke in secret, thus stressing yourself further. You would go out late at night to buy a new pack out of fear that you might soon run out of cigarettes. You would tremble from cravings whenever you didn't have any cigarettes with you. Was this a comfy lifestyle? Think about how much time you would lose while smoking, how it would hold you back from whatever work needed to be done. Think about what discomfort it used to create when you didn't smoke, as it may now too if a craving appears. It will all pass soon enough and you won't have to be enslaved to this "drug" any longer.

Now that you have more free time and you manage to hold temptations at bay, you can preoccupy yourself with improving other aspects of your life. I hope you started engaging in any kind of physical activity by now so that you may keep your metabolic rate at the same level as it was while smoking. If you continue to do any kind of physical active, soon you will, directly and indirectly through it, the person you have always dreamed of when you were little. Don't disappoint your past dreams and take measures in improving your life on all possible levels.

In principle, if you manage to abstain from smoking for about a month you will get rid of any thoughts of smoking. From now on, you shouldn't experience any major cravings. As I noticed, some might still crave a cigarette or two but only because they were never psychologically, emotionally and physically ready to embrace change, but they transitioned from a smoker to non-smoker too sudden. You are now ready. You may have vague memories of smoking because your subconscious might still struggle with its last powers to keep you determined to smoke. It did indeed partly understand that you wish to become, or remain, a non-smoker but it just wants to assure itself that this is true. Assure it further through your persistence and soon enough all these will be problems of the past.

It is very easy to come back to smoking since you have smoked in the past, so watch out not to fall in a trap. You are a firm non-smoker now, don't hazard all the effort you went through for a few ounces of tobacco. If you do try a cigarette out, I can assure you the taste will be horrible, but it will cause further cravings due to the nicotine. Regardless if the taste and smell will be unpleasant, the nicotine will enter your body and it will provoke smoking related memories which will start nagging you on a psychological level as well. Once you do light one up, your mind will think it's ok if it continues to ask for more and more, and in the end you will be addicted once more.

Between two and four weeks it is possible for you to experience fatigue, but your mind won't feel foggy anymore and you won't have an intense desire to eat anymore. Nervousness and the feeling of depression will fade away and you won't cough as much anymore as before when your lungs were trying to remove any residue.

Try not thinking about smoking too much anymore. See it as a strange activity others engage in, rather than something that you used to do. Smoking was a dark period in your life, you can bury it away deep down in your memory and forget about it. Don't give it any more thought, but if you do remind yourself of smoking, try thinking about it positively: I *have* smoked, but now I no longer do so and I'm happy. You are now clean of any toxins, you feel good, you have escaped this vice.

After a month, think about how awesome you are. Not many people manage to get this far, but you did. Take the money you started saving and use it as you imagined when you started. There is no point in talking about the days that will follow. The need for tobacco is extremely low, if it still exists, and it will be only triggered by typical events – friends who smoke, actors in movies. From now on you are a free person and smoking is a thing of the past. You have passed this challenge. Realising this will recover you for a bright future.

YIELDING

I hope it isn't the case for you to give in to smoking. Don't forget, a single cigarette is enough for you to have to start over. The need for tobacco decreases over time, but it will amplify if you smoke a cigarette or even puff a smoke. Nicotine enters the bloodstream instantly. Be firm, don't yield to temptations. Don't hazard all the effort you have so far invested. You have no idea how well a non-smoker life can be until you try and persist in it. Leave any thought that smoking would be better for you aside, don't create any illusions and don't let yourself be influenced by them, they are all lies.

Smokers believe that they smoke because they choose to do so. Because they like it. They remember, vaguely at least, their first puff. But nobody really remembers when they continued to smoke. This is because they haven't really chosen to continue smoking. Addiction came into play. If you have ever tried to quit smoking you have made a right choice. If you continued to smoke it is not because you chose to do so, but because you gave in or have failed to quit. You were overwhelmed by addiction and by the illusion that a cigarette does you good.

If you tried to become a non-smoker with the help of this book and at some point gave in to cravings, don't get sad. You are way stronger than you were before and you simply need to start over. Try tackling the problem with new force by pushing yourself further each time you yield to smoking and re-read the book. It sounds like a productive punishment. You probably didn't believe in yourself and in your capabilities hard enough or you didn't manage to convince your subconscious to fully aid you. It isn't easy. Whoever says it is, doesn't know what you are going through. It is easy only if you follow the steps that need to be taken, presented in this book, the biological and psychological needs and only if you truly wish to become a non-smoker. If you give in to smoking, you didn't truly desire such a new life, so you should revise the reason you gave in and think deeply about the measures that need to be taken further. Ask friends for help if you can't manage to quit on your own. Try analysing with them why you have failed and how they can help you in your next attempt to become a non-smoker.

If you are reading the book for the first time and are just passing by, I must warn you about the possibility of giving in after an attempt to become a non-smoker. A lot of people gave in before succeeding. But why should you prolong the process and torment if you can do it on your first try? Anticipate in advance any reason you might have to give in. After a few days of abstinence, your mind will start looking for ways and reasons to make you smoke again. It will even make up lies that if you have made it so far, you deserve a smoke as a reward. Don't forget that even that one puff can ruin all that you have achieved and it will reset your plan of action. You will have to start over and go through the same things again. Giving in to smoking can affect your morale. At the next attempt to quit smoking, you might believe you are weak and you won't succeed this time either. But this isn't true, simply because you gave in a few times doesn't mean that you won't eventually succeed. Only those that give up for good are truly defeated. Try again and again, learn from your failure and these new experiences will fortify the next attempt to quit.

In case you do give in, try not to start smoking in secret so you won't end up avoiding certain situations or people and ruining your relationship with them. Admit your failure in front of others and tell them to help you. They will surely show compassion and understand you. They won't blame you if you honestly explain what you are going through and that you wish to try again.

Pay attention to your life. Maybe you gave in to smoking due to external pressure. Remember that any stress or problems you may face in life will exist whether you engage in smoking or not. Cigarettes won't remove them, but if you start smoking again you will have another issue to deal with later on. Don't imagine that the problems in life aggravate due to the absence of cigarettes, but by remaining a non-smoker you will have the energy to solve any problem with a clear mind, a healthy and vigorous body. Don't confuse your inner struggles and external issues with the lack of nicotine.

About 76% of ex-smokers relapse because of psychological influencers. Note down the reasons you want to become a non-smoker, if you haven't done so already, and focus upon them. Some give in after a soliciting day. Don't forget that any person, whether a smoker or non-smoker, has bad days in which nothing seems to work right and in which they might feel overwhelmed by panic and anxiety. You don't have to worsen your day by smoking. You can get over such a day even if you don't smoke.

Look on the bright side: it is possible to uplift yourself in such a day knowing that you made it pass without giving in. This could be a motivational factor that can help you solve your issue.

In case you don't manage to quit smoking and you give in to cigarettes after a few attempts, I would like to recommend you another book I wrote: "Learn how to lie and smoke in secret effectively...". It will help you fool the people around you and help you continue smoking without getting caught while ruining your health further, wasting money and preparing yourself for a premature death. God forbid... I was joking. Remove any ambition of continuing to smoke from your mind and open your eyes. There is no sweeter life than the one you can savour with your loved ones. If you don't want to become a non-smoker for your own sake, at least do it for the ones who truly care for you.

DO RESEARCH

I recommend you do some additional study on what it means to smoke, especially upon the process of becoming a non-smoker. Surf the internet for various websites, watch online videos, listen to other ex-smokers' stories so that you may motivate and inspire yourself to do the same. Maybe thus better ideas will follow that match your lifestyle better and that can help you deal with withdrawal. Listen to what others have got to say, what methods they tried. Inspire yourself, but don't forget that each person is different. If someone tells you it was hard for them, it doesn't mean it will be for you too. Maybe he wasn't as researched as you are on the matter and didn't take even half the measures and tips I have mentioned in this book to ease the process. Even the techniques that helped them might vary. For some it may be enough to offer them motivational quotes and to remind them why they want to become a non-smoker, others you need to tie up so they can't smoke.

ENDING REMARKS

After reading this book I am sure you have learned a lot of new information regarding the life of a smoker but even the one of a non-smoker. You should already be eager to stop smoking and to be thrilled by the idea of a new life. If it isn't so, it means that you didn't truly understand the message of this book. I don't mean that you didn't understand what has been written in it, we do both speak English, but that you might have missed the essence of the words and of the presented facts. It is impossible for you to argue that the life of a smoker is far better, pleasant and healthier compared to the life of a non-smoker. If you have such thoughts it means that your subconscious is still fighting to keep you in your comfort zone. Break the barrier and act upon them as there are no real reasons for you to continue smoking. Warning! Don't let yourself be fooled. Your conscious mind might know that it isn't ok for you to smoke and is still struggling to convince the subconscious. Embrace the life of a non-smoker and all its benefits totally, and you will surely succeed.

Re-read the book until you convince your subconscious in aiding you. Talk about the ideas with other people so you can "breathe" further "life" to the words in this book and the information at hand. You have the opportunity to embed the information into your mind. If you fear failure, I can tell you that it is not the case. Many people tried to become non-smoker, have failed, but have tried again and again, until they succeed. They have planted the seeds of knowledge obtained from this book into the garden of their mind until they rose in strong trees, bearing fruits of success, a healthy and stable life of a non-smoker. Try as much as it is necessary. Compared to your previous attempts you now possess more information that can aid you in your future struggle. If you don't succeed on your own, with your own plan, thread on the steps I have taken to succeed in the -7 and + 7 days.

Maybe you have understood everything that is written in this book, how smoking works and how dangerous it is to you. But you still that you would miss out if you became a non-smoker. You don't. This is yet another illusion of the subconscious trying to convince you to continue smoking and to keep you in your comfort zone. It will keep lying to you and creating illusions until you manage to convince him about the truth and that you truly desire to quit. How can you unmask it whenever it disguises itself in a reason to smoke? Easy. Since smoking doesn't have any benefits, any argument or incentive meant to convince you to smoke is a lie, an illusion meant to make you light a cigarette up. I can't explain this easier. When you have such thoughts, you should simply deny them. When you want to light a cigarette up, you stop. Support your positive thoughts consciously and block the negative ones until any cravings pass. Don't let yourself be fooled by your own subconscious mind but rather try fooling it with the help of your conscious mind and the truth. When it conceives a plan for you to smoke, tell it why you would rather prefer to remain a non-smoker by repeating the list of reasons you want to quit for and the fact that you are more happy and fulfilled with your new life. If you don't feel this way, the subconscious is masked in another illusion. It's sly, but you are too, and thus you can defeat it with its own weapons.

If you are reading the book for the first time now, I recommend you read it once more. I know this can be frustrating but this is a perfect way to print everything I wrote into your mind. The process of becoming a non-smoker represents the sum of everything written down in this book. Yes, you can quit by snapping your fingers and deciding not to smoke. You resist withdrawal and after a while everything will be fine. Easy said. We are complex beings with complex thoughts, complex challenges and complex lives. Therefore, we need complex solutions for the transition into the life of a non-smoker to occur smoothly and progressively, and it can so be only if you dedicate yourself to creating it that way.

You will never succeed in achieving something if you sit on a bench and let life pass you by. Those around you will obtain everything you have ever wished. You will simply sit there, full of hate and envy, just because you allow potential to remain potential and you don't accept change – in this case, a change that, regardless from what point you view it, can only be good. Don't sit there like a melancholic masochist observing how everything that is dear to you is being kidnapped from your life by a vice. Act. Take control over your life. Even if you aren't on a big ship, you are at least on a small boat with rows... so row towards your goal like you have never rowed before, until you arrive on the shore and discover the treasure of your life.

BIBLIOGRAPHY

https://www.heart.org
https://www.medicalnewstoday.com/articles/3
19460.php#2
https://www.helpguide.org
https://www.rogelcancercenter.org/
https://www.ncbi.nlm.nih.gov/pmc/articles/P
MC4363846/
https://www.who.int
https://www.ncbi.nlm.nih.gov/pmc/articles/P
MC6358212/
https://www.ncbi.nlm.nih.gov/pmc/articles/P
MC5662490/
https://smokefree.gov/
https://dictionary.cambridge.org/

The Brain: The Story of You (Ed. Vintage,
2017) - David Eagleman
Mapping the mind - Rita Carter (Ed. University
of California Press, 2010)
*The Fitness Mindset: Eat for energy, Train for
tension, Manage your mindset, Reap the results* - Brian
Keane (Ed. Rethink Press Limited, 2017)

The Power of Your Subconscious Mind - Joseph
Murphy (Ed. Simon & Schuster Ltd, 2019)
Super Brain - Deepak Chopra, Rudolph E. Tanzi
(Ed. Lifestyle Publishing, 2013)

Printed in Great Britain
by Amazon